EVERYTHING I KNOW ABOUT
BUSINESS I LEARNED FROM

EVERYTHING I KNOW ABOUT
BUSINESS I LEARNED FROM

SUCCESSFUL EXECUTIVES REVEAL

STRATEGIC LESSONS FROM THE

WORLD'S GREATEST BOARD GAME

by

ALAN AXELROD

RUNNING PRESS
PHILADELPHIA · LONDON

9   8   7   6   5   4   3   2   1

Digit on the right indicates the number of this printing

Library of Congress Cataloging-in-Publication Number 2002100437

ISBN 0-7624-1327-1

Cover designed by Whitney Cookman
Interior designed by Serrin Bodmer
Edited by Greg Jones
Typography: Avenir and Galliard

This book may be ordered by mail from the publisher.
Please include $2.50 for postage and handling.
But try your bookstore first!

Running Press Book Publishers
125 South Twenty-second Street
Philadelphia, Pennsylvania 19103-4399

Visit us on the web!
www.runningpress.com

As ever, for Anita

CONTENTS

PREFACE   11

INTRODUCTION – MONOPOLY 101   13

PART I – There Are Rules   21
Part I is based on the official rules of play and uses them as the basis for lessons in business.

LESSON 1: The Object of the Game   22
What the game is about—according to its makers.

LESSON 2: All Things Being Equal   26
The consequences of starting off on a level playing field.

LESSON 3: A Roll of the Dice   32
The role of luck.

LESSON 4: Passing GO   40
Managing a regular income.

LESSON 5: The Rule of Opportunity   44
The philosophy of acquisition at every turn.

LESSON 6: Facing Reality and Paying Your Debts   51
Balancing needs, wants, opportunity, and resources.

LESSON 7: Mortgaging the Future   56
Using credit.

LESSON 8: Vigilance   64
You snooze, you lose (as in MONOPOLY, so in life).

LESSON 9: A Random Walk   70
What can you expect each time around the board?

LESSON 10: The Taxman Cometh   76
Tax strategies.

LESSON 11: On Sitting It Out   84
The pluses and minuses of JAIL and FREE PARKING.

LESSON 12: The Virtue of Shortage   89
Exploiting a little-used feature of the game: the housing shortage.

LESSON 13: Let's Talk   95
Exploiting another under-used feature: the player-to-player trade.

LESSON 14: Going Once . . .   103
Auction time.

LESSON 15: Kicking over the Bench   108
Bankruptcy (and the Alamo defense).

PART II – And Then There Are *Your* Rules   113
Part II goes beyond the official rules to focus on tips and nuances of play that have much to teach about success in the larger game that is business.

LESSON 16: The *Real* Object of the Game   114
Don't try to win. Just make everyone else lose.

LESSON 17: Psych (Or, Who's the Shlub Who Chose the Shoe?)   122
Using your token and theirs to psych your opponents.

LESSON 18: Gain the World *and* Lose Your Soul?   130
The role of ethics.

LESSON 19: Hell Is for Nice Guys   134
Committing to ruthlessness.

LESSON 20: Cornering Corporate Karma   138
Committing to cooperation.

LESSON 21: Luck Is the Residue of Design   146
Playing the odds.

LESSON 22: The Smartest Properties to Own   152
What to buy and why.

LESSON 23: The Dumbest Properties to Own   159
What to avoid buying and why.

LESSON 24: Cash Cows and Old Sows   163
The tried, true, and resolutely unglamorous.

LESSON 25: Pit of Vanity   168
Don't work from emotion.

LESSON 26: Start-up Strategies   173
Smart moves at the beginning of the game.

LESSON 27: Turning the Corner   178
Developing a winning strategy at mid game.

LESSON 28: Winning the Endgame   184
On being a closer.

LESSON 29: The Limit of Greed   192
How far will this engine get you?

SOURCE INDEX   199

PREFACE

In business these days, games are serious business. The 2001 Academy Award winner for best picture, best director, best supporting actress, and best screenplay, *A Beautiful Mind*, is about the mathematician John Nash, whose pioneering work in applying game theory to economics and negotiation earned him a Nobel Prize. Today, business seminars abound in how to use game theory—and, specifically, games like MONOPOLY—to model real-life business scenarios and situations.

This book is not such a seminar. It steers well clear of theory and instead accelerates at full speed into reality—the reality that is bounded by the MONOPOLY game board as well as the reality beyond it. Even more important, it explores the space between those two realities, the provocative, revealing, and surprisingly useful connections between MONOPOLY and business.

I am hardly alone in the belief that games in general and MONOPOLY in particular model business. In fact, I feel rather like the would-be inventor who comes up at long last with the Big Idea only to find the Big Idea suddenly popping up everywhere he looks and, somehow, suddenly expressed by a multitude of flapping lips and wagging tongues. Once it was firmly lodged in my own mind, the notion of holding up to business the mirror of MONOPOLY suddenly seemed to be everywhere. That is, in the remarks of others, I kept stumbling across the lessons about business I assumed MONOPOLY had taught me and me alone.

Well, if you can't beat 'em, quote 'em.

And so you will find in this book my own analysis of what we might call the "great MONOPOLY metaphor" presented in counterpoint to the insights, observations, and, in some cases, confessions of CEOs, executives, entrepreneurs, economists, deal makers, and students of business— some from the past, most very active today, all remarkably successful.

Everything I Know about Business I Learned from MONOPOLY is not a how-to-win-MONOPOLY handbook, although you will find a good many winning strategies and tactics to apply to the game. It is, rather, a handbook on how to use this brilliant, addictive, ruthless (and, incidentally, fun) game to think about, to explore, and to rethink the nature of business and the doing of business. What I mean to say is this: Like all books that aspire to be useful, *Everything I Know about Business I Learned from MONOPOLY* offers nothing more than an insight and a provocation—a starting place. You know, GO.

— Alan Axelrod

INTRODUCTION:
MONOPOLY® 101

The world is filled with people who've never played MONOPOLY. But it is also true that, since 1935, about 200 million MONOPOLY sets have been sold worldwide. Most of these, presumably, have been purchased by families, which means that you have to multiply this 200-million figure by three, four, or more to get an idea of just how many people have played the game at least once. And playing MONOPOLY is a lot like snacking on potato chips: nobody can play just once.

So, okay. There are plenty of people in the world who have played MONOPOLY and who continue to play MONOPOLY. It's still only a game, right?

"I started playing when I was four," said James Mallet, the 1983 U.K. MONOPOLY Champion. "I learned to count on it, learned to read on it, and learned to lose on it, so it's helped me to grow up!"

An unusual and extraordinary experience, right?

Actually, it's much more usual and ordinary than you'd think. The scientific name for Human beings is *Homo sapiens*, which literally means "wise man" or "knowing man." In 1938, the renowned Dutch philosopher-historian Johan Huizinga wrote a book in

Chance Business is a game, the greatest game in the world if you know how to play it.

—Thomas J. Watson, Sr., founder and president, IBM

which he argued that *Homo sapiens* were rapidly evolving into an even higher level of intelligence. He called the book—and the species—*Homo ludens*, or "playful man." What most sharply distinguishes humans from other animals, Huizinga and many others have argued, is their need and ability to play, to model reality with games, and to think of reality in terms of play.

Over the ages, parents have told children some pretty foolish things: *The world is flat. The sun orbits the earth. Life is serious. Work is hard. Now, stop playing and get down to business!*

Some few of us manage to outgrow our parents' well-meaning "wisdom." You'll meet some of these people in the pages that follow. They include some of the top executives and CEOs of the world's most successful businesses, as well as the people who study them and document their work. These executives are for the most part people who—lucky for them—never learned to separate work from play. For them, work is fun. But it is also true that they take fun seriously. Whether in the arena of business or at the MONOPOLY board, they play in earnest.

THE MAGIC OF MONOPOLY®

Parker Brothers began to distribute the board game MONOPOLY nationwide in 1935, and it was an instant hit. By the end of its first year in large-scale production, it had become the best-selling game in America.

Just what magic chord had it struck in the popular imagination?

In 1935, America, like the rest of the world, was deep in economic depression. The New Deal of President Franklin Roosevelt had brought some emergency relief and a measure of hope, but it had not proved a panacea. Business, the marketplace, and capitalism itself were just not working the way they were supposed to. Companies were going belly-up.

People were out of work. Families were losing their farms and their homes.

Then along came a game that modeled capitalism, that created a world in which people received salaries, where properties were bought and sold, taxes were levied, landlords were paid, money was made, and money was lost. Some players got richer, some poorer, and in the end, all players would go bankrupt save for one: the winner. And this game of free-flowing capital and financial risk, in the depths of an economic depression, became a bestseller of unprecedented magnitude.

TITLE DEED
PACIFIC AVE.

MONOPOLY is like business because the goal is to win, and winning requires understanding the value of a flexible strategy, of asset-ownership, of risk-taking and having the foresight to make your own luck.
—Len Roberts, Chairman and Chief Executive Officer RadioShack Corporation

Consider the classical Greek philosopher Aristotle's explanation of the appeal of great tragic dramas—plays like *Oedipus Rex* and *Medea*—in which incredibly painful and horrific things happen while the audience experiences fascination and pleasure at the spectacle. Aristotle explained that tragedy gives fear shape and meaning, so that the audience comes through it cleansed, purged, and generally feeling better. In life, scary things are scary in large part because they contain so much that is unknown. In drama, the action has a definite contour, a beginning, a middle, and an end. Things may be scary, but the system works. Events are given a recognizable and familiar form and format. Besides, when it is all over—and we know that it will all come to an end—we get up out of our seats, leave the theater, and go home.

Maybe the Depression-era success of MONOPOLY can be explained by something like Aristotle's idea of tragedy. To be sure, the game offers the opportunity to become a wealthy capitalist, the owner of railroads, of utilities, of real estate developments. But, even while offering the possibility of fantasy wealth, it presents the prospect of all-too-familiar failure. When you can't pay your taxes, your bills, and, most of all, your rent, you lose everything in bankruptcy. You're out of the game. In an era of carefree Busby Berkeley movie musicals and escapist songs like "We're in the Money," who wanted to think of a fate like this?

Apparently, a lot of people did.

Just as a great tragic play allows the audience to live safely through the heights and depths of human existence—to share that experience while sitting cozy and comfortable in a plush theater seat—so MONOPOLY allowed Depression-ridden Americans to experience financial success and failure all in the pleasant and familiar company of friends and family. People were not only willing to face reality, but had a good time doing so, because the reality of MONOPOLY was governed by rules and, like any good drama, had a beginning, a middle, and an end. It was neither mindless nor escapist. Far from it.

Here was a game that modeled capitalism at its most ruthless, a game in which everyone loses—except for one. For every Rockefeller or Morgan, there were, after all, hundreds of thousands selling apples in the street or standing in a bread-line. Yet MONOPOLY was a game, which meant that it made sense in a way that life didn't always. It was easy to understand, and while it is true that much in MONOPOLY depended on luck and the roll of the dice, much could also be controlled, manipulated, and managed. And that—the feeling of control, of being the master of one's fate—was, during the Depression, even harder to come by than cash and a decent job.

Community Chest

Actually, I played MONOPOLY before I could read—at four years old. Selling things was kind of in me.

—Steven Peskaitis, CEO, Lexon Technologies

THE EVOLUTION OF MONOPOLY®

The world has been playing MONOPOLY for nearly seventy years. No wonder we take it for granted. But think for a moment about the enduring popularity of the game, and you begin to realize what a truly remarkable achievement MONOPOLY is. Every day, modern economists produce models of the real world that are without doubt more intricately accurate than the world of MONOPOLY. Yet few of us would derive much pleasure "playing" with these models. In MONOPOLY, we have a strikingly realistic model of the real world, yet the authentic details of that model never overshadow the game. MONOPOLY is just complicated enough to be both realistic and fun. It is feasible fantasy. It invites us to play with reality. It is, in short, one of the very few genuinely great games that have ever been invented.

Now, what genius could have invented it?

It was a dream and a piece of oil cloth. In 1933, Charles B. Darrow played a game on oil cloth on his kitchen table, fell in love with the game's exciting promise of fame and fortune, produced his own version and sold them one by one to friends and family. When demand for the game grew beyond his ability to fill orders, he brought the game to Parker Brothers who first rejected it on the basis that the company's experts indentified 52 design errors.

Undaunted, Darrow continued to produce handmade editions on his own and was highly successful. Parker Brothers caught wind of the success and decided to buy the rights to the game. In 1935, owned by parker Brothers, the MONOPOLY game became America's best-selling game, and the rest is history!

THE APPEAL AND INFLUENCE OF MONOPOLY®

The "game" Darrow had played, which led to his development of

MONOPOLY, was actually created years earlier as a more serious educational and political endeavor. That game, though embraced by and improved upon by numerous business school professors and students, never really had a commercial appeal. But Darrow saw its true potential and developed it with the general public in mind.

All told, MONOPOLY had evolved over the course of three decades before Darrow, beginning not so much as a game but as an exhibit in support of a new theory of taxation—a rather sober-sided model of economic reality. It was conceived originally not by a game manufacturer or a toy maker, but by students and teachers of economics. And only later was successfully commercialized by a hungry salesman living in desperate times. From the beginning, MONOPOLY was the product of economic reality and was more a genuine business model than a toy. If it succeeded as a game—and wildly so—it is because its several inventors understood that the reality it modeled was itself very much like a game.

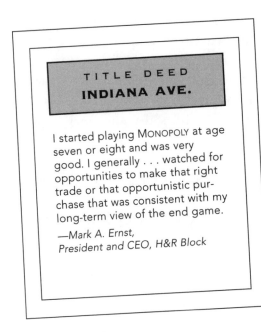

TITLE DEED
INDIANA AVE.

I started playing MONOPOLY at age seven or eight and was very good. I generally . . . watched for opportunities to make that right trade or that opportunistic purchase that was consistent with my long-term view of the end game.

—Mark A. Ernst,
President and CEO, H&R Block

The appeal of some games are as fantasy. They set up a world apart from our own. The appeal of MONOPOLY, however, is not as a world apart, but as a microcosm, a miniature of the business world that, in varying degrees, is familiar to all of us.

In fact, many top executives and experts who rule and report on the business world today got their first taste of this world in their younger days, by playing MONOPOLY. And as you'll see throughout this book, their various philosophies regarding business-world success—what it is, how to achieve it, and how to hold onto it—mirror and mimic the strategies necessary to win at the board game. If we can learn anything about business from these accomplished and astute experts, then we can learn from one of their primary sources—the game of MONOPOLY. Which, by definition, should be a more fun way to learn.

Unfortunately, it's so easy to get so serious about doing business that business ceases to be fun, and when it stops being fun, it stops being creative. Fortunately, it's also easy to get serious about MONOPOLY. And it is precisely when you get the most serious about this game that it becomes the most fun. Go ahead. Get serious. Have fun. Go!

PART I:

THERE ARE RULES

A lot of business books tell you that the surest way to lose at the game of business is to play by the rules. We're not about to tell you to cheat at MONOPOLY. (Where's the fun in that?) But by the time you've finished this book, you'll see that there are rules, and then there are *your* rules. You don't master MONOPOLY—or the business world it models— by failing to think beyond and in addition to the rules. However, before you can use the official rules of MONOPOLY as the foundation upon which to build your own game, you need to understand those rules, how they affect play, and how they relate to the game as a microcosm of the wider world.

For a game some thirty years in the making, involving the work of many hands, including those of trained economists, the rules of MONOPOLY are remarkably few and elegantly simple. There are classic games, such as the ancient Asian game of Go, with even fewer rules, but in the case of Go, the real trick is determining just when the game is over. No such problem with MONOPOLY. The object of the game is clearly stated in the little rule sheet that is packed with each MONOPOLY set:

"The object of the game is to become the wealthiest player through buying, renting and selling property."

In Part II of this book, we'll explain how this statement, straightforward and beyond dispute as it may seem, is somewhat misleading. But we need to save that for a little later in the book, when it's time to stop talking about "the rules" and begin pondering "*your* rules." First, we need to make sure that we've fully thought through the implications of the object of the game as given in the official rules.

BEHOLD THE TORTOISE

Whatever else the 1960s were, they were a time of wall posters featuring cute pic-

Chance

First get in, then get rich, then get respectable.

—Bernie Eccleston, British billionaire and CEO, Formula One

tures captioned by "clever" mottos. You saw them in offices, in kitchens, and in teen and pre-teen bedrooms. You may recall the Peanuts gang's poster entitled "Happiness Is a Warm Puppy," cartoonist R. Crumb's famous "Keep on Truckin'," and that ubiquitous image of a kitten hanging by its front paws from a tree branch over the legend, "Hang in there, baby."

Chance

Winning is everything. The only ones who remember you when you come second are your wife and your dog.
—*Damon Hill,*
British Formula One driver

Also popular was an image of a lone tortoise accompanied by a caption that went something like this: "Behold the tortoise. He gets nowhere unless he sticks his neck out."

Now, for most of us, our first encounter with MONOPOLY was as an all-American "family" game, something out of a Norman Rockwell painting, strictly *Leave it to Beaver* stuff, and possibly even served up with mom's apple pie. The game emerged from a world of comforting Americana, its simplicity reminiscent of Ben Franklin's simplistic wisdom found in such phrases as "early to bed, early to rise . . ." and "a penny saved is a penny earned."

But as you grow up with MONOPOLY and play the game more and more, you sooner or later learn to leave the Ben Franklin wisdom behind and embrace something more akin to the poster parable of the tortoise. If the stated object of MONOPOLY is "to become the wealthiest player through buying, renting and selling property," you'll never win by saving your pennies. You have to stick your neck out.

You have to pony up to buy, rent, and sell.

RECKLESSNESS OR CAUTION?

He who owns the most when he dies, wins.
—Ivan Boesky, American financier

The stated object of MONOPOLY requires players to be aggressive in acquiring property.

But does aggressiveness invite recklessness?

Well, while it is irresponsible to advise a player to be reckless, the fact is that if you must choose between extremes—either recklessness *or* caution—you are far more likely to win through recklessness than through caution.

Later, we will consider in detail questions of cost versus benefits, but, all other things being equal, it is the nature of MONOPOLY to buy and to buy aggressively. True enough, the relentlessly aggressive approach can lead rapidly to bankruptcy, but it can also bring victory. In contrast, the cautious approach can keep you in the game longer—before you are finally and at long last victimized into bankruptcy—but unless the other players are extraordinarily unlucky, caution is not a winning strategy.

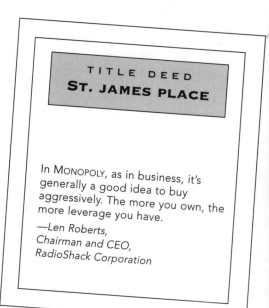

TITLE DEED
ST. JAMES PLACE

In MONOPOLY, as in business, it's generally a good idea to buy aggressively. The more you own, the more leverage you have.
—Len Roberts, Chairman and CEO, RadioShack Corporation

The stated object of MONOPOLY is acquisition. The game, therefore, is not about preserving or husbanding resources. It is about acquiring more—and not for the static purpose of possession, but rather to reach the dynamic goal of forcing others into relinquishing their resources to you. MONOPOLY is a dynamic game. It compels us to contemplate the true cost of competitive business: what you do, you do at the expense of another. The purpose of acquiring property, of becoming the wealthiest player, is so that you may extract resources from the other players, "cost" them, and, ultimately, cost them the game. Bye, bye, mom and apple pie.

MONOPOLY shares with most games a feature so common that you might not think it even worth mentioning, let alone thinking about. In MONOPOLY, everyone begins at the same starting line—GO—and with the same amount of cash—$1,500. That is, all players begin at the same place and with the same resources. Hardly an innovation. Indeed, the level playing field is such a familiar feature of games that we take it for granted. It is the unusual, exceptional game that alters this situation, typically by introducing the concept of the handicap, as when the better golfer gives the lesser opponent the benefit of a few strokes.

CONSIDER THE LEVEL PLAYING FIELD

We've said that a big part of the appeal of MONOPOLY, a reason for its longevity and an important element in its thirty-

year genesis as a finished product, is the striking authenticity with which it mirrors and models the real world. Yet one thing that immediately sets MONOPOLY apart from the real world is the perfect equality that prevails before the first move is made. We live in a nation dedicated to the proposition that all men are created equal, but, of course, we know that this equality is a matter of right and law, not a case of economic and cultural advantage.

Take two sample business careers:

John Richman is born into a well-to-do family. His mother is a corporate vice president, his father a high-powered attorney. Young John is sent to the best private schools and, at home, he is frequently exposed to enthusiastic and knowledgeable conversation about business, making money, and investing money. When it comes time for college, John gets a fine Ivy League liberal arts education, followed by a premium MBA.

Community Chest

Equal opportunity means everyone will have a fair chance at becoming incompetent.

— Laurence J. Peter, American business theorist

Thanks to a combination of his parents' connections and his schooling, he lands a terrific job on the corporate fast track and is the head of a major division well before his thirtieth birthday.

The family of Sally Middling is working class. Her childhood certainly isn't impoverished, but her father always seems just able to make ends meet as a computer-repair technician. Sally's mother takes on part-time work from time to time, but mostly she thinks of herself as a homemaker. The family doesn't talk much about business or careers. Sally goes to the local public schools and then on to a community college. She finds work with a temp agency for a while, then lands a job as an executive assistant.

THE GHOST OF CHRISTMAS YET TO COME

These outcomes aren't particularly surprising, given the unequal starts each of the "players" had. However, they aren't inevitable. Consider the moral of Charles Dickens' classic novel, *A Christmas Carol*. When the Ghost of Christmas Yet to Come reveals to Ebenezer Scrooge his grim future, the old man quite correctly asks if what he has been shown are things as they *must be* or as they *may be* if he fails to reform in the here and now. The ghost does not answer him, but *we* know the answer. His fate will be his own doing.

Similarly, our own fates are in large part decided by our actions and not completely by our starting points.

History is littered with stories of rich boys and girls who were given all the advantages but who grow into failures.

Belly up to the local bar. . . .

"He's a self-made millionaire," says one of the patrons, making an observation regarding a certain businessman.

"Yeah," responds the smart alec sitting on the next barstool. "He inherited $20 million and made it into a million."

But history—especially business history—is also peppered with tales of those who really did make it on their own. The late and much-loved Dave Thomas of Wendy's Hamburgers fame is a prime example. A poor orphan at the start of his life, Thomas nevertheless built an empire, burger stand by burger stand,

Community Chest

Everybody's got the will to win, but it's only those with the will to prepare that do win.

—Mark Cuban,
Owner, Dallas Mavericks

beginning with just one restaurant. It's the American dream, as outlined in the popular nineteenth-century rags-to-riches novels of Horatio Alger.

Experience tells us that, in the real world, early advantages are indeed helpful, but they are no guarantee of coming out a winner. And some would even say that those who have had life served to them on a silver platter actually start off with a disadvantage. They have fewer opportunities to acquire and develop the aggressive skills necessary for survival. They are by definition less creatively desperate and productively hungry than folks born into more humble circumstances. In short, they lack ambition—precisely because they have never needed it.

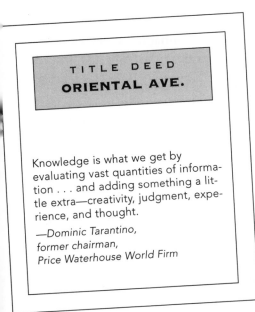

TITLE DEED
ORIENTAL AVE.

Knowledge is what we get by evaluating vast quantities of information . . . and adding something a little extra—creativity, judgment, experience, and thought.

—Dominic Tarantino,
former chairman,
Price Waterhouse World Firm

THE FORTUNE FACTOR

Such points could be argued endlessly. The significant matter here is that how one starts off may shape and influence where one ends up, but it does not determine it. Such factors as innate talent, attitude, experience, and luck play huge roles in the game of life and in the world of business.

While MONOPOLY fails to model the real world in that every player starts off with the same resources, the game still provides ample space for the exercise of what's inside each player, allowing each to draw upon talent, attitude, and experience. As for luck, this intangible is incorporated into the MONOPOLY world in the way countless games introduce it: with a roll of the dice.

Like most games, MONOPOLY has no difficulty modeling real-world chance. The dice bring into play a convenient random element. However, MONOPOLY takes the role of luck one step further, by also introducing two decks of cards: COMMUNITY CHEST and, of course, CHANCE. For the casual player, the opportunities, instructions, and penalties printed on these cards are quite literally products of the luck of the draw. As we will see in *Lesson 21: Luck Is the Residue of Design*, the more serious and committed players see beyond the apparent randomness of the cards. They learn to exercise a degree of control over these cards.

BRING IT

The operation of sheer chance aside, the initial level playing field of MONOPOLY serves to concentrate and intensify all the skills and attitudes that each player brings to the game.

The appeal of many games is, in part, the way they mirror real life. Who can deny, for instance, that football, in some measure, is a battle and mirrors a real military contest? Yet in real battles, one side often has better weapons or enjoys the advantage of holding the high ground or occupying a formidable fortress. If part of the appeal of a game is how it models life, another part is how it *differs* from life, by eliminating many of life's messy and distracting inequalities, so that the skills, intelligence, strength, and character of the players emerge cleanly and clearly as the most important elements in the contest.

A good game eliminates the variables that are no fun and brings into play only those that have inherent drama, excitement, and truly enduring—because of their truly personal—significance.

MONOPOLY strips each player of external advantages and liabilities. It allows and it compels each participant to bring to the game board only what's inside.

Do the players really start off equal?

On second thought, of course they do not. Some come to the game smarter, some are hungrier, some are stronger. And some discover, in the course of play, how to become smarter, hungrier, and stronger. Like all great games, MONOPOLY both tests who you are and provides the space in which you may become someone even better.

Luck. Some people believe in it, others tell you there's no such thing. Just about everyone who's made it in business warns that, whatever luck is or is not, you can't count on it, and you certainly can't build a career on it.

THINKING ABOUT LUCK

The assumption that you cannot build a career on luck is doubtless all too true. Interestingly, most of us just don't give much thought to the subject of luck. Let's think about it now.

First: The word *luck* and the concept it denotes are too often used interchangeably with the word *chance* and the concept *it* denotes. "Luck" implies the existence of some controlling power, force, or influence behind visible entities or events—some *thing* that pulls the strings. "Chance," in contrast, connotes nothing more or less than mere randomness. Even those who deny the existence of "luck" as some sort of palpable entity admit that chance is ever present in all that we do.

Community Chest

Preparation is everything. Noah did not start building the ark when it was raining.

—Attributed to Warren Buffett, American entrepreneur and financier

Second: Even if you accept the existence of chance and the role that it plays, don't be too hasty to turn your back on the concept of luck. Now, we're not talking anything supernatural here, but maybe we *are* talking a little Latin. In the *Aeneid*, the Roman poet Virgil (70-19 B.C.) observes: *Audentes fortuna iuvat*— "Fortune favors the brave."

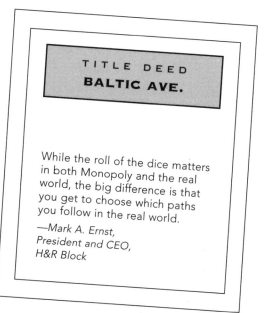

While the roll of the dice matters in both Monopoly and the real world, the big difference is that you get to choose which paths you follow in the real world.
—Mark A. Ernst,
President and CEO,
H&R Block

Hold that phrase (in Latin or English) in your mind, and think about some "lucky" people you know. Almost certainly, they are not the foot-scraping, hat-in-hand, meek and mild types. Almost certainly, they project an aura of confidence, a can-do attitude, and even boldness. There is a chicken-and-egg question in this. Do the fortunate appear confident and bold because they've been lucky, or is their "luck" in some measure the product of confidence and boldness? Virgil, for one, thought the latter.

FORTUNE FAVORS THE BRAVE

Boldness and confidence do not guarantee good luck. As the old pirate-movie song goes (in *basso profundo* voice): "Many brave hearts are asleep in the deep." And while you don't have to rummage very long through the annals of history and literature to find a quotation like "Fortune favors the brave," the chances are good that you'll first encounter "Discretion is the better part of valor" and "Better to turn and run away and live to fight another day."

Yet there is no denying that bravery and boldness are simply more compelling, more desirable, more *attractive* than caution, let alone cowardice. We admire the confident and the decisive, and we look to them for leadership. If we are drawn to them, it is because they are *attractive*. For this reason, the brave tend to be successful. They are the leaders, the managers, the commanders. They are the successful persuaders, the young CEOs who capture the attention of the investment capitalists, the innovators who rivet the focus of the marketplace, the entry-level assistants who quickly rise to the level of account executive and beyond.

PLAYING IT BRAVE

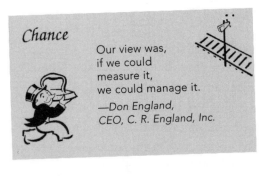

Chance

Our view was, if we could measure it, we could manage it.

—*Don England, CEO, C. R. England, Inc.*

How does the approach of the brave transfer to the narrow confines of the board game of Monopoly?

At first glance, although Monopoly clearly models the real world in many respects, play does not seem to call for the kind of leadership qualities just mentioned. After all, Monopoly isn't a team game.

Or is it?

It is possible for a single, ruthless, determined player to virtually ignore everyone else in the game and still win. But this approach arbitrarily discounts valuable assets the game contains—namely, the other players. As we'll see in *Lesson 13: Let's Talk*, Monopoly offers many opportunities for player-to-player deals. *Lesson 20: Cornering Corporate Karma* goes even further, exploring the potential power of alliances between players.

Who will make the best deals? Who will make the most powerful alliances? The timorous and hesitant, or the bold and decisive? In MONOPOLY, as in the larger arenas of life and business, it pays to be "attractive," to possess the power of the brave in order to draw others into supportive alliances with you.

Even beyond the utility of bravery as an aid to closing deals and mustering allies, the bold approach has a great positive effect on you yourself. Confident people anticipate success. They design themselves and all of their plans to accommodate it. They expect it. Naturally, this does not guarantee success, but, just as naturally, it creates a better fit between the individual and the *prospect* of success. Put it this way: If you feel like a winner, you will behave like a winner, and if you behave like a winner, you will most likely make more of the moves a winner makes. You will, therefore, improve your—let's just say it—*luck*.

THINKING ABOUT CHANCE

Now, we've just discussed luck and have suggested an attitude that will help generate it. In Part II of this book, *Lesson 21: Luck Is the Residue of Design* will go a step further and present ways in which you can squeeze some good luck out of apparently random chance. For now, though, take a moment to ponder the topic of chance in and of itself.

The world of game enthusiasts is sharply divided between those who profess a preference for "games of chance" and those who favor "games of skill." Roulette is as pure an example of a game of chance as you are likely to find, and chess is a good example of a game of skill. However, most games actually fall somewhere between the extremes of chance and skill.

Take MONOPOLY. It calls on the player's judgment, her ability to assess a financial situation, and her deal-making skill and savvy, and yet it is also propelled by a roll of the dice. What could be more random than a pair of dice tumbling across a table with the promise that they will soon land face up?

The roll of the dice, we've pointed out earlier, simply and elegantly models in MONOPOLY the element of chance that enters into any life, any career, and even any particular day lived in the world beyond the game board.

In fact, the roll of the dice models chance more profoundly than may at first be apparent.

Anyone who deals with mathematics or statistics at a reasonably advanced level appreciates how difficult it is to generate a truly random number. Of course, common sense tells us that randomness should be the easiest thing in the world to achieve. Do you want randomness? Just put a bunch of numbers in a hat and pick one!

But the fact that the number of numbers in the hat is finite makes true randomness impossible in this case. Indeed, one of the most challenging tasks computer programmers face is the creation of "random number" generating programs, programs that, in effect, tap into infinity to create something at least approximating true randomness. So far, no one has ever come up with a program capable of generating truly random numbers.

Consider this question: Who among us experiences true randomness in the course of a day? We get up from what is probably a familiar bed, in a familiar house, among familiar people, and take a familiar route to work, where we do a job that is, for the most part, filled with familiarity. Sure, there may be surprises. We may oversleep. We may spill coffee

Community Chest

If you do it right 51 percent of the time you will end up a hero.
—Alfred P. Sloan, former president, General Motors

down the front of our only freshly pressed shirt. Unexpected highway construction may force us to make a detour on the way to the office. And, once at work, we may be faced with some brand-new, unexpected task. But even in a day that's chock full of surprises, the surprises occur in a context of the familiar, the expected.

In life, the element of chance does not propel our existence into the realm of anarchy any more than the roll of the dice makes MONOPOLY an experience of utter randomness. The comforting fact is that only so much can happen in MONOPOLY. You can't arbitrarily pass and re-pass GO. You can't decide to collect $200 on one passing of GO and $2,000 the next time around. You can't invent new streets and properties to buy. You can't move backward and forward at will. The rules of the game, like the familiar parameters of your life, limit the possibilities *within which* chance operates.

PLAY BY THE NUMBERS

Even the roll of the dice, like drawing numbers out of a hat, presents finite possibilities and, therefore, embodies chance without also embodying pure randomness. Hardcore players of Craps—the dice game at the center of *Guys and Dolls* and any number of tough-guy detective novels—commit to memory dice charts that illustrate the numbers of ways in which a player can throw a given total with two dice.

It works like this:

"Dice" is the plural of "die." Each die is a small cube sporting spots—called "pips"—that total a number from one to six on each face of the cube. Adding opposing faces always yields seven. For instance, opposite the face with six pips is the face with one pip (six plus one equals seven); opposite the five-pip face is the two-pip face (five plus two equals seven); and finally, opposite the three is the four (three and four are seven). Because each die has six sides and MONOPOLY is played with two dice, there are thirty-six combinations that can be made—six times six—generating totals of two through twelve.

Nothing random here. Only thirty-six throws are possible. Of these thirty-six throws, it is very easy to calculate how many of the possible throws will result in a given total:

1 of 36 throws will yield a total of 2
2 of 36 throws will yield a total of 3
3 of 36 throws will yield a total of 4
4 of 36 throws will yield a total of 5
5 of 36 throws will yield a total of 6
6 of 36 throws will yield a total of 7

Let's pause. Of all the totals possible in a roll of two dice, seven is most likely, because there are six ways to make this total: 6 and 1, 1 and 6, 5 and 2, 2 and 5, 4 and 3, and 3 and 4. (In contrast, there is only *one* way to roll a two: 1 and 1.) Think of the rolls from two through seven as taking a trip down the side of a pyramid, with each step getting lower and easier: two ways to make three, three ways to make four, four ways to make five, five ways to make six, and, at the base of the pyramid, six ways to make seven. From seven onward, you labor up the pyramid:

5 of 36 throws will yield a total of 8
4 of 36 throws will yield a total of 9
3 of 36 throws will yield a total of 10
2 of 36 throws will yield a total of 11
1 of 36 throws will yield a total of 12

With this pyramid in mind, the random quality of the dice roll diminishes. It becomes possible to predict the likelihood of throwing a particular number. If you have your heart set on BOARDWALK, you've got a good shot at it on your next throw if you're six, seven, or eight spaces away from it, but it's a long shot indeed if you're two spaces away or twelve.

Knowing the pyramid does not diminish the role of chance in MONOPOLY, let alone eliminate it, but it does reduce the perception of randomness by allowing you to be something more than a passive witness to the roll of the dice. This fact will go a long way toward giving you more confidence, which, in turn, should lead you to experience more "luck," as noted above.

KNOWLEDGE AS A FORCE MULTIPLIER

Armed with knowledge of the *non*-randomness of the dice, you can then plan each move and make each decision with at least a modicum of foresight and judgment. This in itself gives you an edge over the other players. But such knowledge also supplies what military strategists call a "force multiplier," which is a weapon or other asset that produces more effectiveness than is immediately apparent. Getting a leg up on randomness not only gives you a tangible and quantifiable edge, it allows you to ratchet up that intangible quality called confidence—boldness and bravery—which fortune so greatly favors.

Three lessons, then, to take *away* from the MONOPOLY board, are these:

1. In all ventures, take steps to reduce randomness.

2. Counter chance with knowledge.

3. Create luck with self-confidence built on understanding.

Passing GO and getting paid is one of the great pleasures of MONOPOLY, as it is of life. Most of us are raised with the belief that "making a living" means getting a good job with a good salary and a regular paycheck. Typically, as we're growing up, anything else is made to seem a longshot, a risk, maybe even a careless self-indulgence. In a sense, then, that GO square in MONOPOLY reflects and reinforces good old American workaday wisdom: get a steady job, collect a steady paycheck, hold tightly to your fringe benefits, and make the payments on your picket-fenced bungalow.

In a sense, the game of MONOPOLY reflects that received wisdom, but *only* in a sense.

"NO MAN HAS ENOUGH SALARY"

Uncle Charlie, a character in Arthur Miller's classic play *Death of a Salesman*, observes, "No man has enough salary."

Community Chest

Game theory is a significant part of senior management education.

—Dallas Luby, executive vice president, General Reinsurance

What Uncle Charlie says has profound spiritual reso-nance—"Man does not live by bread alone" and all that—but, in MONOPOLY, such a saying has a more immediate and practical application. It is true that the $200 you get every time you pass Go is part of MONOPOLY, which means that the notion of a regular salary is also part of the game. But another message is loud and clear: You can't get by on that $200 alone.

Chance

Expenditure rises to meet income.
—C. Northcote Parkinson, British political scientist

You need to do more than collect a salary. You need to risk investment in property and construction. Fail to do this, and you are sure to lose. This applies directly to the game of MONOPOLY in all cases, and to the game of business and personal finance in most.

SURVIVAL OR SUCCESS?

Successful business people understand salary much the way that good players of MONOPOLY understand Go. Salary is about subsistence and survival. To get beyond this basic level in business, you need to get beyond mere salary. You need to put money at risk, and you need to do so with strategic aplomb. Thus, while MONOPOLY provides a comforting echo of what mom and dad told you about landing a "good, solid" job or learning a "good, solid" trade, the game ultimately pushes you far beyond the cozy comfort of what you can expect come payday.

ISLAND OF CERTAINTY, SEA OF RISK

Yet Go does figure importantly in play, and it should form a part of your game strategy. The Go payday is the closest to a sure thing MONOPOLY gives us. It is certainly possible to miss a payday, as when you draw a Go TO JAIL card (which includes the unfortunate directive, "Do not pass GO. Do not collect $200," alas). It is also possible to pass "Go" only to land on INCOME TAX immediately thereafter. ("Oh, what's the use? Just leave the $200 in the bank.") On the other hand, you may be directed to "Take a ride on the READING (RAILROAD)" or "Advance to ST. CHARLES PLACE"—in either case, collecting an unanticipated $200 if, in the process, you pass GO.

Most of the time, however, GO means nothing more or less than a dependable $200 each trip around the board. At any point, you know where you are on the board, and you certainly know where to find GO. Based on these two pieces of information, you can more accurately estimate the risks involved in straining your cash flow to purchase a property or to do some building. In a game where much is left to chance, the winning strategy involves eliminating as much of the uncertainty as possible. Anticipating GO is one element that reduces the quantity of unknowns. Such a reduction should bolster your resolve to take risks.

READING RAILROAD

A 31-year-old real estate agent, Jacobs appreciated the value of investing in real life as much as in the MONOPOLY game.

—Philip Orbanes, author of The Monopoly Companion, On 1983 Monopoly World Champion Greg Jacobs

WITHIN YOUR MEANS

In life beyond the game board, salary represents a kind of bottom line. Most of us need to live within the constraints of a salary. Ambitious folk work hard to increase their salaries. A relatively few truly inspired people find alternatives to salary in entrepreneurial activities of various kinds.

With respect to salary, MONOPOLY does not model real life very closely. While living within one's salary can be a viable—if possibly dull, limiting, or at least constraining—option in life, in MONOPOLY, it is an impossibility. You cannot win on salary alone.

Great games are liberating, providing an arena in which you can take risks that you would not venture in life. In MONOPOLY, you can experience the adrenaline rush found at the brink of bankruptcy without endangering your child's present orthodontic needs or future college education.

Community Chest

Money is like manure. If you spread it around, it does a lot of good, but if you pile it up in one place, it stinks like hell.

—Clint W. Murchison, American entrepreneur and financier

But even in this anxious and exciting arena, you have the modest haven offered by the knowledge that a brand new $200 is ready and waiting for you just around the corner.

"How about a nice, relaxing game of MONOPOLY?"

Not an unwelcome invitation, to be sure, and, doubtless, there are many people who find MONOPOLY comfortable in its familiarity and, therefore, relaxing.

These people, however, are not the players who win.

A RULE IGNORED

For the serious player, which means the player committed to winning, MONOPOLY is hardly a "relaxing" game. It is a dynamic experience, requiring close attention and calling for continual decision making. Except for brief interludes in FREE PARKING or JAIL, the action does not stop.

Chance

Buy everything you land on.
—Bill Forbes, 1984 U.S. Monopoly Champion

This may come as news to the surprising number of people who don't adhere fully to the rules of the game. You know who you are. You land on a property, you choose not to buy it, and then . . . the turn passes to the next player as you reach at your leisure for another potato chip.

Wrong!

Under "Buying Property," the rules of MONOPOLY unambiguously state that, having landed on an unowned property, "If you do not wish to buy the property, the Banker sells it at auction to the highest bid-

Chance Seize opportunity by the forelock and see where it leads you.
—Armand Hammer, founder and CEO, Occidental Petroleum

der." Yet it is astounding how many players choose to ignore this provision. Some do so consciously and deliberately, claiming that it's a bad rule or a rule that is only for purists, because to auction every unbought property, in their estimation, makes the game too long. But most players who ignore the rule do so thoughtlessly. If questioned on the issue, they typically reply that this "is the way they learned to play" or this "is the way we've always played it in my family."

Many unauthorized departures from the official rules—especially the downright criminal practice of feeding fines and taxes into a "kitty" that is then reaped by anyone who lands on FREE PARKING—are similarly ascribed to some vague body of tradition as nameless as it is, apparently, sacred.

As we have already learned, the rules of MONOPOLY are the product of a thirty-year process of invention, evolution, and refinement. Indeed, the *personal* "rules" we introduce in *Part II* of this book do not presume to alter in any way the *official* rules of the game. Why not? Because none of the improvised, traditional, and unofficial practices people have added over the years improve play. If you are one of the many who do not allow the Banker to auction off unsold property because "that's the way we've always played," consider Ralph Waldo Emerson's warning that "a foolish consistency is the hobgoblin of little minds." In other words, you should start questioning the wisdom of doing things a certain way because that's the way you've always done them.

THE DYNAMISM OF MONOPOLY®

Here's why it's important to put unsold property up for auction: Doing so keeps play dynamic. And dynamism is the essence of MONOPOLY.

It is one of the aspects of the game that so vividly models life in general and business life in particular. There is no still point, no rest, no relaxation—until victory or bankruptcy. There are decisions to be made and deals to be sealed. Played correctly, the pace of MONOPOLY should be brisk, verging on frenetic.

Think you'd rather relax? Well, consider this: Each unowned property you land on is an opportunity for profit (that is, for costing other players their money). Each unowned property that goes up for auction spreads the opportunity around. In a typical business day, how many genuine opportunities come your way? How about in a week? In a month? In a *year*? What is more exciting or gratifying than experiencing a span of a mere two, three, or four hours in which opportunities come at you fast, furious, and continually? It's a rush! If you want to relax, oh, go pick up a fishing rod.

Chance

Risk is what an entrepreneur eats for breakfast. If you have no appetite for this stuff . . . then get out of the game right now.

—Heather Robertson, author of Taking Care of Business

THE OPPORTUNITY EQUATION

An uninterrupted stream of opportunity aimed only at you would be like a steady diet of chocolate mousse—too much of a sweet thing. It would also take the dynamic quality out of the game. The dynamism of MONOPOLY is also propelled by a potent equation: the principle that every opportunity you pass up becomes one for another player. That is, providing everyone is aware of and is playing with the auction rule in full effect.

Your decision not to buy CONNECTICUT AVENUE means that someone else has the opportunity to buy it—and not just if she happens to land on it three, six, or seven moves in the future, but immediately, at auction. However, if you fail to play by the auction rule, a significant portion of the energy drains from the game. While the opportunity you've passed up doesn't die, it becomes dull and dormant until someone else lands on that property.

Without auctions, the stakes of the game, the demands of the game, are greatly diminished. And to diminish the demands is to diminish the fun. What's also diminished is MONOPOLY's compelling power as a model of capitalism. For the auction gets to the heart of that.

Too often, we view our lives and careers through tunnel vision. What we really need is something like *ecological vision*. When biologists view the natural world, they see it as an interdependent system in which all parts have an affect on each other and the whole. An organism does something here, and various other organisms are affected there. In business, what you do and what you choose not to do may affect you immediately and individually, but it also prompts any number of other people to do or refrain from doing any number of things. Each action or inaction affects the ecology of the business landscape in which you exist.

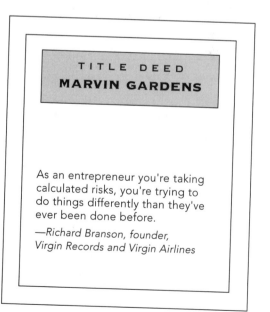

TITLE DEED
MARVIN GARDENS

As an entrepreneur you're taking calculated risks, you're trying to do things differently than they've ever been done before.

—*Richard Branson, founder,*
Virgin Records and Virgin Airlines

CREATING NEW OPPORTUNITY

There is another twist to the auction rule, which you will find in the official rules of the game: "Any player, including the one who declined the option to buy [the property] at the printed price, may bid." This means that you may land on a property, decline to buy it, then, when it is put up for auction, you may join the bidding to get it for a bargain price. Of course, you may be outbid—or, if you are unexpectedly caught in a bidding war, you may actually decide to bid more than the price printed on the TITLE DEED rather than lose the property. This is the kind of chance you can choose to take—or not to take—based on your knowledge of the other players, the milieu of the game at hand, and your own confidence level.

THE RULE OF OPPORTUNITY

Throughout this book, you will find rules of thumb and strategies for helping you to evaluate opportunities. These are helpful in MONOPOLY; that is, they have helped the winners to become the winners. Many of the rules and strategies also have application beyond the game board. Yet you can ignore all the advice you find here and still play a good many winning games—*if* you hold onto one "rule," the Rule of Opportunity.

It is this: Unless you have a positive, purposeful, affirmative reason to say No, say Yes to every opportunity that presents itself.

Given the opportunity, buy every property that still holds the possibility of becoming a monopoly. The only occasion on which you might choose not to do this is if you are in immediate danger of bankruptcy.

Next, given the opportunity, purchase a property to prevent another player from acquiring a monopoly. If Joe has two green properties, and you land on PACIFIC AVENUE, which he does not yet own, buy it. Yes, this is a sacrifice, but it is a valuable one. Besides, it gives you a powerful bargaining chip, should you ever want to make a deal with Joe.

Those are the easy decisions, and many players know to make these almost instinctively. More difficult is deciding what to do when you land on properties where blocking another player's monopoly is not an immediate issue and the prospects for your building a monopoly are slim.

If, for example, Joe owns one green property and Donna owns another, should you buy PACIFIC AVENUE when you land on it?

If you are flush with cash and already have one or two very good monopolies yourself, it is probably a good idea. On the other hand, you may choose to let it go to auction, reasoning that the others won't find it terribly attractive, either, so that you can acquire it at a bargain price. Of course, if you are very short of resources, it may be better just to let it go altogether.

Chance

Only through curiosity can we discover opportunities, and only through gambling can we take advantage of them.

—Clarence Birdseye, founder, Birdseye

But don't be too hasty in this decision. PACIFIC AVENUE is priced at $300. Now, look at the title deed. The property can be mortgaged for $150. If you can buy it for less than $150, you gain valuable collateral indeed. This is leveraging at its very best.

THE TAKEAWAY

In the next lesson, *Lesson 6: Facing Reality and Paying Your Debts*, we will give further consideration to managing your money. And in *Lesson 22: The Smartest Properties to Own* and *Lesson 23: The Dumbest Properties to Own*, we will provide more detailed guidance on what to buy, when, and why. But, for now, the takeaway lesson is this: Resist the impulse to relax. Be alert to opportunity, and don't be terribly particular about distinguishing one opportunity from another. Seize whatever you can whenever you can. The opportunities you fail to capitalize on become the opportunities—and properties—of someone else, usually instantly.

It's a good thing MONOPOLY is so much fun, because it's a game parents love while being something that they are willing and actually eager to play with their kids. We all know that most amusements parents feel comfortable with for their children's entertainment are by definition pretty boring for the parents themselves.

GETTING REAL

But let's get real. As far as kids are concerned, what board game can possibly compete with the interactive action, adventure, blood, gore, and pulsating stereo sound effects offered by a computer-based first-person shooter game?

And since we're getting real, please note that the question just asked is not entirely rhetorical. It's true that, in MONOPOLY, you don't puree your opponents with a "rail gun" or annihilate them with a "photon torpedo." But, if

Community Chest
Anybody who runs a successful high-tech company has to be an eternal optimist, has to be able to take big risks.
—John Sculley, CEO, Apple Computers

you're playing MONOPOLY to win, you do try—and try very hard—to destroy your opponents financially and to drive them out of the game so that you alone are king of the hill.

Electronic shoot-em-ups draw on a different set of skills than MONOPOLY requires, but a commitment to ruthlessness is a key element shared by both games. This is something most parents either fail to realize or, if they happen to be very good MONOPOLY players in addition to being parents of junior MONOPOLY players, they choose to overlook. To choke back an ecstatic gloat over taking his firstborn's last $1,275 when the unfortunate lad lands on PACIFIC AVENUE, Dad says to himself: *This game is a lesson in handling money. It teaches financial responsibility. Joey overextended himself, and so he suffered the consequences. This is good for him. He's learned a valuable lesson.*

Chance

Nothing defines human beings better than their willingness to do irrational things in the pursuit of phenomenally unlikely payoffs.

—Scott Adams, creator of Dilbert

But is that what Joey really learned? More important, is that what MONOPOLY really teaches?

RISKY BUSINESS

At a basic level, as a game involving buying and selling, spending and collecting, MONOPOLY does indeed impart some of the fiscal facts of life, including the one that Charles Dickens's hapless Wilkins Micawber so memorably uttered in *David Copperfield*: "Annual income twenty pounds, annual expenditure nineteen nineteen six, result happiness. Annual income twenty pounds, annual expenditure twenty pounds ought and six, result misery."

But if fiscal responsibility were the main object of MONOPOLY, well, there wouldn't be any MONOPOLY, because you can't make a very interesting game out of staying cautiously within your means.

MONOPOLY teaches the risk of taking risks. Risk and win, result happiness. Risk and lose, result misery. (But, then, you *can* always play again!) The point of this, however, is not to learn to avoid risk, but to accept risk as necessary to success. Having accepted the necessity of risk, the object becomes making a choice of what risks to take and how far to take them.

Community Chest With every dollar we get in our hands, we hold the power to choose our future to be rich, poor, or middle class.

—*Robert T. Kiyosaki, author of Rich Dad, Poor Dad*

That is, accepting a risk should not require abandoning fiscal responsibility. If, growing impatient in the course of a long game, you decide on the kamikaze strategy of mortgaging yourself to the hilt to acquire, say, the Boardwalk-Park Place monopoly and quickly build on it in the hope of making a quick killing, you might win. But, if you're completely tapped out, you'll more likely be forced into bankruptcy before anyone lands on the properties.

Putting all your chips on a single number is a risk, maybe you can even call it a calculated risk—but it is not a *wisely* calculated risk.

A DEFINITE MAYBE

We've established that MONOPOLY is not about saving money. MONOPOLY is about risking money—intelligently. *Winning* MONOPOLY is also about risking money—intelligently *as well as* aggressively.

Does the "winning MONOPOLY" model translate successfully into managing one's business and career in the world beyond the game board? The answer is a definite maybe. What is certain is that it does not provide a *foolproof* business and career model. There is no guarantee that aggressively accepting even a well-informed risk will advance you. It may result in a total blowout.

A BANG OR A WHIMPER?

In MONOPOLY, failure to take intelligent, aggressive risks may or may not avoid a blowout, but it almost always ensures a slow leak that, eventually, will leave you just as flat.

What about real life? In this arena, the scrimpers and savers can, in fact, be happy. Yet Henry David Thoreau's chilling observation—"The mass of men lead lives of quiet desperation"—rings true, as does the plight of T. S. Eliot's poor J. Alfred Prufrock, a lonely wimp who "measured out his life with coffee spoons."

AND SO WE LEARN . . .

The takeaway lessons seem to be these:

First: In MONOPOLY as in life, reaching foolishly beyond your means will very likely result, as Mr. Micawber observed, in misery.

Second: Stretching intelligently but aggressively to the edge of your means is often necessary to win in MONOPOLY. In life, the stakes are much higher, of course, and the consequences of each risk both much greater and, alas, usually more permanent. Nevertheless, the aggressive

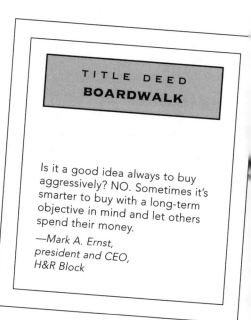

TITLE DEED
BOARDWALK

Is it a good idea always to buy aggressively? NO. Sometimes it's smarter to buy with a long-term objective in mind and let others spend their money.
—Mark A. Ernst, president and CEO, H&R Block

but intelligent risk is a part of living, working, doing business, and making deals.

Third: In MONOPOLY, the failure to take risks almost certainly ensures that you will lose. But what about in life? There are probably plenty of people—no one knows how many—who are reasonably and even unreasonably content to live fully wrapped within their means, no matter how modest those means may be. These people shun risk. Are they losers? Are they winners? Or are they something else?

Fourth: Parents often say they like MONOPOLY because it teaches kids something about the "value" of money, about handling it "responsibly," and about "living within your means." Yes, the game does provide kids (and adults, too, for that matter) a kind of financial "flight simulator" in which to learn and to try out the lessons of value, responsibility, and prudence. But the far more compelling lessons of the game are those that expose as illusion the sense of safe haven that comes with avoiding risk.

To shrink from risk in MONOPOLY is, really, to opt out of the game itself—not that this kind of opt-out saves you from losing. On the contrary, as we've said, consistently avoid risk and you will almost certainly lose in the end. It's just that you'll do so with the melancholy sense of never really having played the game at all.

It would be truly reckless and rash to declare flatly that this lesson of the game precisely models a lesson found in the real world. But, at the very least, MONOPOLY alerts us to the inescapable risk of *avoiding risk*—that is, a career, an enterprise, perhaps an entire life that just goes flat, however gradually.

Is there a soul alive in the Western world who has not seen—and seen more than once—Frank Capra's 1947 film *It's a Wonderful Life?* You remember how it ends. George (Jimmy Stewart) Bailey's bumbling uncle has mislaid $8,000 from the family-run Building & Loan company, and the perennially self-sacrificing George is about to take the fall as an embezzler—until practically the entire town of Bedford Falls shows up in his living room with cash to lend or give: many thousands more than the missing eight grand. George, overwhelmed, discovers that his guardian angel Clarence has left him with his favorite book, an original edition of Mark Twain's *Huckleberry Finn*, which Clarence has inscribed: "No man is poor who has friends."

Community Chest

You borrow money at a certain rate and invest it at a higher rate and pocket the difference. It's that simple.

—*Roberto Goizueta, former CEO, Coca-Cola Company*

CREDIT SQUEEZE

Well, it *is* a wonderful life, but, in MONOPOLY, your friends can do absolutely nothing for you. Toward the end of the official rules sheet found in each game is an innocent-looking heading: "MISCELLANEOUS . . ." What follows it is a rule that is both important and frequently overlooked or deliberately ignored:

"Money can be loaned to a player only by the Bank and then only by mortgaging property. No player may borrow from or lend money to another player."

In MONOPOLY, both player-to-player benevolence and loan sharking are not merely discouraged, they are prohibited outright. Players' credit options are limited, severely, to a single channel: bank lending secured by a mortgage. There are no unsecured loans in MONOPOLY.

THE MORTGAGE GAME

In life away from the game, getting a mortgage can be a complicated, tedious, nail-biting, and hair-pulling ordeal. In MONOPOLY, it's quite simple. Unimproved properties can be mortgaged at any time. No haggling or negotiation is necessary—or, for that matter, allowed. The "Mortgage Value" is printed right on the property deed. It is one half the property's purchase price *as printed on the game board* (not the auction price, if the property was acquired at auction). You just turn the property deed to its flip side and collect the cash from the bank.

Simple as this is, there are three important catches.

First, the word "unimproved" is key. Only a property devoid of houses or a hotel can be mortgaged. If the property you wish to mortgage is already built up, you must sell back to the bank, at half price, *all* of the buildings on *all* of the properties of the mortgaged property's color group. That is, for example, if you want to mortgage ILLINOIS AVENUE and you have two houses on it and two each on the other red streets, INDIANA and KENTUCKY AVENUES, you have to sell all six houses, at a 50 percent discount, to the bank. Only then can you collect your mortgage money. (Note that only the unimproved property is mortgaged. The funds you get from the houses and/or hotels are proceeds of a sale and yours to keep.)

Second, you cannot collect rent on mortgaged properties or utilities. Fortunately, however, there is a bit of a break here. Let's say you've mortgaged ILLINOIS AVENUE; you can't collect rent on it, but you can continue to collect rent on the other two reds, INDIANA AVENUE and KENTUCKY AVENUE. Of course, these no longer have buildings on them—you've sold them back to the bank, remember?—so the rent is on the paltry side. Nevertheless, because you still own all three red streets, the rent is based on the monopoly price: "If a player owns ALL of the Lots of any Color-Group, the rent is Doubled on Unimproved Lots in that group."

Chance

If you are scared to go to the brink, you are lost.
—John Foster Dulles, former U.S. Secretary of State

Third, the mortgage money costs you. You lift the mortgage by paying back to the bank the mortgage amount plus 10 percent interest. If you've mortgaged more than one property in a color group, you must pay off the mortgages on all of them before you can begin rebuilding on your monopoly. You do catch one very significant break in all this, however. In contrast to a real-life mortgage, the MONOPOLY mortgage is not dependent on time. There are no monthly payments to make, and you choose the moment when the loan comes to maturity. Indeed, it is perfectly possible for the game to end—even with you as the winner—without your having paid off all of your mortgages.

BUYING AND SELLING MORTGAGED PROPERTY

A surprising number of players overlook the fact that mortgaged properties can be bought and sold. The player who owns a mortgaged property may sell it to another player at whatever price the two agree on. The new owner acquires not only the property asset, but the mortgage liability as well. He is not obliged to lift the mortgage immediately—although he may do so, if he chooses, by paying the bank the mortgage due plus 10 percent interest. If he does not lift the mortgage at once, he still must immediately pay the bank 10 percent interest. Later, when he does decide to pay off the mortgage, he must pay 10 percent in addition to the 10 percent he had paid when he first bought the property.

THE MORTGAGE AS A TOOL OF OPPORTUNITY

Some players look upon mortgaging as strictly an emergency measure—something to be avoided unless you are truly up against the wall. This is an unnecessarily puritanical or, at least, overly conservative (not to say wimpy) policy. Business, both public and private, runs on borrowed money. Borrowing creates necessary cash flow, giving you the flexibility to do what you need to do when you need to do it or when the time is ripe for doing it.

This doesn't mean you should approach mortgaging carelessly. In fact, of all the moves and operations that are part of MONOPOLY, borrowing money requires the most thought. Put it another way: The player who thoughtlessly acquires properties has a better chance of winning than the player who thoughtlessly acquires properties *and* thoughtlessly borrows to acquire them.

Chance

By definition, risk-takers often fail. So do morons. In practice it's difficult to sort them out.

—*Scott Adams, creator of Dilbert*

WHAT TO MORTGAGE

Prioritize what you choose to mortgage. Begin with single properties—especially of color groups in which you have little or no hope of acquiring a monopoly. For instance, if Joe owns CONNECTICUT AVENUE and Mary owns VERMONT AVENUE, both light blues, your light-blue ORIENTAL AVENUE looms as an apt candidate for a mortgage. There's very little else you can do with it, except collect the occasional $6 in rent. Mortgaged, it nets a quick $50.

Except when you are in a jam or when you are presented with a great opportunity, you should avoid mortgaging a property from a group that has monopoly potential, especially if you already own two of the properties in a three-property group.

Even more costly, of course, is mortgaging a property that is already part of a monopoly. We've just explained why. You can't build on a monopoly if one property in that color group is mortgaged. If you have already built on a monopoly, you must sell to the bank, at a steep 50 percent discount, all of the buildings on all of the properties within the color group before you can mortgage any property in that group.

THE "ELECTIVE" MORTGAGE

Sometimes you have little choice about mortgaging. You're strapped, and you've landed on BOARDWALK with a hotel. But remember to look at mortgaging not just as a parachute, to be used only in case of disaster, but also as a positive tool by which you can pry open opportunity.

How do you know when to take out an "elective" mortgage—not a bail-out loan, but a loan to enable an opportunity?

If by mortgaging single properties, you can raise enough cash to significantly help you build a monopoly up to three houses per property, you should seize the opportunity. As Philip Orbanes points out in his book *The Monopoly Companion*, you should also mortgage single properties if this will help you to build hotels on the light blue or the purple group. Achieving anything less than these levels of development presents a highly questionable justification for *electively* mortgaging even lonely single properties.

Once you shake off your puritanical anti-borrowing scruples (assuming you have any), you may be tempted to test the other extreme: foolish fiscal aggression.

Let's say you find yourself in a game in which other players have already amassed some pretty high-powered monopolies. You will feel a strong urge to mortgage to the hilt in order to develop whatever you can, even if it's the lowly purple group or the almost as lowly light blue. Doing this may make you feel better for the moment, but it is almost certainly a futile gesture that will drain your resources so that, when you finally do land on one of your opponent's big-time properties, you'll go bust in an instant and find yourself sitting out the rest of the game. Of course, if the game is drawing to a close anyway, and you have few prospects for the long term, it may make good sense to go for broke by mortgaging everything in sight. Just bear in mind that, when you go for broke, you very likely will, in fact, go broke.

Chance On business: This isn't rocket science; we've chosen one of the world's more simple professions.
—Jack Welch, former CEO, General Electric

PAYBACK TIME

Some people just hate owing money. In MONOPOLY, it's best to get over this feeling. Don't rush to pay off your mortgages. It is generally best to hold off until you have extensively developed whatever monopolies you have. What does "extensively" mean? On all but the purples and the light blues, you should have a minimum of three houses on each property before you even *think* of paying back the bank. In the low-rent district, make sure you have hotels before you start flipping title deeds right-side-up.

Generally, it is a good rule of thumb to pay off mortgages in the reverse order from which you mortgaged them. But don't be rigid about this. If lifting a mortgage on INDIANA AVENUE *right now* means that you can develop a new red-group monopoly *right now*, do it, regardless of the

order in which you had mortgaged the properties.

TACTICS

In *Lesson 3: A Roll of the Dice*, we learned that MONOPOLY, even though so much rides on what the dice do, is less dependent on randomness than may be immediately apparent. In *Lesson 9: A Random Walk* and *Lesson 21: Luck Is the Residue of Design*, we'll further investigate how to make apparently arbitrary choices more informed and effective, and how to actually design good luck rather than simply hope for it. Here and now, however, let's anticipate a bit of Lesson 9.

With the exception of ILLINOIS AVENUE, NEW YORK AVENUE, and BOARDWALK, the street properties nearest GO have the lowest chances of being landed on. Therefore, consider these close-to-GO properties as sources of mortgage money to be tapped in preference to other, more productive properties.

Mortgage single street properties before you mortgage a single utility. A single utility commands higher rent than a single street property. For the same reason, mortgage a single utility before mortgaging any railroads. The return on a railroad is better than the return on a utility— unless the railroad's mortgaged, in which case you collect nothing.

Remember that the overriding object is to borrow money when it makes sense to do so—but always save your cash cows.

BIFOCAL VISION

If you think this discussion of mortgages in MONOPOLY is more technical and more nitty-gritty than most of what has preceded it in this book, you're right. After all, how can you talk about mortgages without getting technical?

But, remember, this book is less about how to play MONOPOLY than it is about how playing MONOPOLY can help you model what you do in business. And so there is a bigger point to this discussion than figuring out what to mortgage and when to mortgage it in a game of MONOPOLY, no matter how hotly contested.

To be sure, the business of business is making money, but it is also managing and manipulating money. MONOPOLY beautifully models both of these functions of business. Acquiring and developing properties makes money, while mortgaging these properties is a key aspect of managing and manipulating money. To focus on one function and to neglect the other is to invite failure—at worst a meltdown; at best any number of missed opportunities.

Paying attention to *management* and *manipulation* calls for a commitment that differs from a determination to *make* money. As reflected in the game of MONOPOLY, the commitment to management and manipulation requires a willingness to roll up your sleeves and run the numbers. It calls for hands-on management, not broad-stroke theorizing and strategizing.

"God," the architect Mies Van Der Rohe once said, "is in the details." If you ignore these details or try to rise above them by delegating the "scut work" to others, then you risk slighting at least half the business of business.

Playing the game—whether it be that of business or MONOPOLY—is exhilarating, and the details should never get in the way of the passion. But try to bear in mind that successful play is guided with bifocal vision, an eye on tactics, and an eye on strategy.

LESSON 8:
VIGILANCE

Good MONOPOLY players are committed to the game. That means they don't just while away their time at the board; they genuinely compete. And when people compete, emotions can run high—surprisingly high.

THE RULE OF VIGILANCE

Want to prompt a red-hot expletive out of your opponent's mouth? Don't count on it happening just because he lands on your BOARDWALK property with its shiny red hotel. That event will elicit a groan from some and, from others, a cry like that of a wounded animal. But a nasty word? Probably not.

No, the way to incite a good, solid curse—or maybe even start a fight!—is to land on your opponent's property, keep silent, draw a poker face, let the next player roll the dice—and *then* say: "You know, I just landed on your property."

If the inattentive property holder knows the rules, the expletive will explode at this point, followed by a shake of the head, and possibly even some hair pulling (his own). Then play will resume. If he doesn't know the rules, however, he won't swear, but, instead, will say something like, "Oh, yeah. You owe me twenty-four bucks."

Of course, the last thing you need to do is to reach down into your pile to fork over the cash. You have better options than that.

But let's assume you're not one to gloat. So, without gloating, you answer this request for your dollars by reaching for the rules and, in an even tone of voice, read aloud: "The owner may not collect the rent if he/she fails to ask for it before the second player following throws the dice."

Now cometh that choice monosyllable—or two.

SNOOZE AND LOSE

Owner inattentiveness is common when a single, unimproved property is landed on. Slack players forget they own ORIENTAL AVENUE or maybe even the READING RAILROAD. In contrast, monopoly properties, with houses or hotels, are usually eyed jealously. Not much chance of catching someone napping in this case. But it does, on occasion, happen. So say you land on ILLINOIS AVENUE, and your little pewter car has to find a place to park within the crowd of four houses. Technically, you owe the tidy sum of $925. But, believe it or not, the owner says nothing before the next player throws.

When you point out what happened, you may elicit painful self-accusation: "*Why* am I so, so stupid?" Or you may produce an excuse such as: "This stinking allergy medicine! I'm half asleep." You may, however, get a brave show of stoic resignation: "Ohhhh . . well."

Chance

There is no resting place for an enterprise in a competitive economy.
—Alfred P. Sloan, president, General Motors

Or, a more genial opponent may offer as a rationalization a taste of modern folk wisdom, such as: "Oh, well. You snooze, you lose."

You may even trigger unexpected maturity: "Well, the rules are the rules."

Or you might just have a fight on your hands: "*What?* That's not fair! Just because I didn't say anything? Come on. What kind of rule is that? We never play by that rule. No one does, except maybe lawyers."

How do you avoid hard feelings in this situation?

Some players just clam up. You land on the property, the owner says nothing, play continues, and you keep quiet, never pointing out what happened.

There are at least three things wrong with this approach:

To begin with, it's a delaying action only. Sooner or later, the owner will figure out what happened, and he will be even more angry than if you had called him on it right away. The reason? He'll feel you've put one over on him.

Second, your not opening your mouth probably won't put off the revelation for long. Another player—most likely the one who rolls the dice next—will point out what happened. Just hope she doesn't say anything until after she rolls, because if she elbows the owner before she rolls, he still has a chance to ask for the money. Rules, after all, are rules.

This brings up a vexing side issue. You observe that Joe lands on Jane's property. Jane fails to ask for her rent. Joe passes the dice to you. Do you roll in silence? Or do you first remind Jane to collect her rent?

Viewed from one perspective, this is a test of friendship. Does your deepest loyalty lie with Jane or Joe? But such a perspective can lead only to agony and accusation. Besides, you have nothing to gain by opening your mouth at this point. If you prod Jane, Joe will be justifiably annoyed with you. If you keep silent, well, you can claim—again, justifiably—that the transaction is between Joe and Jane, and is none of your business.

The rules say nothing about the duty of one player to wake up another. So cling to the rules, and say nothing. On the other hand, avoid grabbing the dice and throwing them in great haste. While you may not want to help Jane, you don't want to give the appearance of aiding Joe, either. Keep the pace normal. Then, after you roll, avoid being the one to break the bad news to Jane. That is the province of Joe. If *you* point out to Jane that she's missed a rent payment, you'll end up looking like a co-conspirator in Joe's plot to cheat Jane out of what's due her. And Jane may just want to kill the messenger as well as the perpetrator.

Community Chest

Nothing focuses the mind better than the constant sight of a competitor who wants to wipe you off the map.

—*Wayne Calloway, CEO, Pepsico*

THE "NICE" ALTERNATIVE—AND WHAT'S WRONG WITH IT

Now, on to the third thing wrong with trying to let sleeping dogs lie. Doing so makes you, at best, mean-spirited and, at worst, a liar.

At some point, it is likely that the owner will recognize his failure to claim the rent due: "Did you realize you landed on my property?"

What will you answer? If you say, "*Yes, but it was up to you to say something about it,*" you'll come off sounding mean of spirit. If, instead, you reply, "*No. Really?*" you'll be a liar. Neither response is worth the price.

There is, of course, another alternative.

You land on Jane's property. She says nothing. You say: "Jane, didn't you notice? I owe you $24."

There is nothing in the official rules of MONOPOLY that explicitly bars you from nudging your opponent in the ribs like this, but doing so certainly violates the spirit of the rules. An important element of

MONOPOLY, part of the way in which it models business life, is that each player takes responsibility for his or her actions and for managing his or her funds and properties. To take on this responsibility successfully calls on an important skill, which MONOPOLY continually tests and challenges: vigilance.

By the time play reaches mid-game, a whole lot is going on. A lot of properties are owned, and some are up for grabs. Players must display all of their title deeds openly, so that everyone can see them. When you land on an unowned purple property, for instance, you should not have to ask, "Does anyone own any purples?" It should be visible to you and everyone else. Before you make your purchase, you scan everyone's title deeds. That's vigilance.

And it is also vigilance to know what you own and to remember to demand your rent when someone lands on what you own. Effective play requires keeping your eyes open and your mind alert.

Perhaps you think of yourself as a charitable person, a nice person, a friendly and helpful person. No game, you believe, is worth getting anyone upset or angry. So, when you land on Jane's property and she says nothing, you nudge, and now you feel kind, warm, cuddly, and, gosh darn it, *nice*.

But you aren't helping your opponent. At the moment, the two of you are in the world of MONOPOLY. You are either in the game or not. If you are in the game, you play the game, and part of the game is maintaining vigilance.

Chance

Winners are people who have fun—and produce results as a result of their zest.

— Tom Peters, American author and business consultant

The rules forbid your lending money to another player. They don't prevent your pointing out that you owe money. However, the same spirit applies. Just as you don't lend money to another player who's short on cash, you shouldn't lend vigilance to one who's short on that commodity. To do so takes you both outside of the world of the game.

Chance

I want to be at the table as a player when they move the pieces around in America.

—Rupert Murdoch, CEO, News Corporation

TOUGH LOVE

Success in living, as well as success in business, requires any number of resources and skills. Few of these can be given or loaned from one person to another. The overwhelming majority has to be acquired and developed on one's own. Crutches are no substitute for a good, strong pair of legs. MONOPOLY asks us to stand on our own two legs, and, if they're not strong enough to support us, we either give up and lose or we work on them, build them up, develop them, and *make* them work.

All truly competitive undertakings require the acquisition and development of our own resources. Victory cannot be borrowed, nor can it be loaned (no matter how "nice" you are). That's the game.

LESSON 9:
A RANDOM WALK

In 1973, maverick investment guru Burton Malkiel wrote *A Random Walk Down Wall Street*, in which he argued that no investment professional or scientific economist could predict stock prices in the short run; therefore, an investor was about as well off allowing a blindfolded monkey to pick his stocks as he was to pay a professional broker or analyst to do the job.

Critics of Malkiel's book stopped right there—with the apparently flawed notion that the market was random and so the best approach to investing in it must likewise be random. Such criticism was wrong-headed, because Malkiel had said no such thing; however, the title of his book did leave him vulnerable.

Chance If you don't know where you are going, you will probably end up somewhere else.

—Laurence J. Peter, Canadian author and business theorist

THE RANDOM WALK DEFINED

In mathematics and statistics, a "random walk" is the problem of determining the probable location of a point subject to random motions. The usual classroom example of this problem is a drunk who starts out from a point (presumably a tavern) and walks one unit of distance for each unit of time. If he weren't drunk, it would be easy to determine where he'd end up after a given span of time, because his direction would be a straight line. But he's a drunk, which means that he staggers forward, back, and from side to side, all unpredictably, randomly. The problem is to find, after some fixed period of time, the probability distribution of his distance from the point of origin.

TRULY RANDOM, TRULY RARE

This is a problem of true randomness. But true randomness, which seems plentiful, is actually not all that easy to come by, especially not in the human-made world. Malkiel didn't argue that the stock market operated in a truly random manner. Quite the contrary, his thesis was that the stock market is "fundamentally logical." The market, Malkiel wrote, "eventually corrects any irrationality—albeit in its own slow, inexorable fashion. Anomalies can crop up, markets can get irrationally optimistic, and often they attract unwary investors. But eventually, true value is recognized by the market, and this is the main lesson investors must heed."

Community Chest

The general who wins a battle makes many calculations. . . . The general who loses a battle makes but few calculations.

—Sun-tzu, Chinese military theorist (c. 500 B.C.)

How to heed it? Malkiel suggested that the small investor was best off buying and holding index funds rather than individual securities or actively managed mutual funds. Index funds are mutual funds that are not actively managed, but instead operate by specific and clearly defined—or predefined—rules of ownership. These rules are set from the beginning, fully known, and not subject to change. When stocks are within the rules of ownership, they are purchased and held. When they no longer meet the rules, they are sold. No other decision is necessary or permitted. Since, according to Malkiel, in the long run, the stock market is logical, investors who buy and hold according to an indexed rule will come out ahead.

RANDOM? OR JUST COMPLICATED?

We are not here to advocate or condemn Malkiel's approach to investing. The point is that he refused to equate the appearance of randomness with genuine randomness and, instead, looked for an order within a very complex, very dynamic, and therefore *apparently* chaotic system.

In *Lesson 3: A Roll of the Dice*, we began to do the same with MONOPOLY by looking at what crap shooters already well know: Chance based on a finite number of possible outcomes (the roll of a pair of dice, each with only six sides) is far from random. But how does this translate to the ongoing action of MONOPOLY? To look at the colorful game board, with its forty squares, you'd think that it was impossible to make even an educated guess about where you might land next. Even if you have in your head the odds of rolling a seven versus a two, how can you put this information to work meaningfully? That is, even if the progress around the board isn't truly, mathematically, a "random walk," isn't it close to being one? After all, in practical terms, how many numbers and calculations can your brain hold? Besides, MONOPOLY is a game. It's supposed to be fun. You shouldn't have to transform yourself into a human computer or go into training as an insurance company actuary just to play the game.

The good news is that you don't have to become an android or an actuary to play MONOPOLY at a better than random level.

Let's pause a moment for a reminder. The book you are now reading is about MONOPOLY as a model for business life. While it may incidentally help you to become a better MONOPOLY player, it is by no means intended to be a MONOPOLY manual. Fortunately, such a manual does exist. It is *The Monopoly Companion* (New Second Edition), by "MR. MONOPOLY as told to Philip Orbanes." In this book, MR. MONOPOLY has done the math, which we can summarize here:

PROPERTY	CHANCE OF LANDING EACH TRIP AROUND BOARD
DARK PURPLE	24 PERCENT
LIGHT BLUE	39 PERCENT
LIGHT PURPLE	43 PERCENT
ORANGE	50 PERCENT
RED	49 PERCENT
YELLOW	45 PERCENT
GREEN	44 PERCENT
DARK BLUE	27 PERCENT
THE RAILROADS	64 PERCENT
THE UTILITIES	32 PERCENT

In the book, Orbanes uses these percentages as part of an overall picture illustrating the return on investment for each property—something we'll get into in *Lesson 22: The Smartest Properties to Own* and *Lesson 23: The Dumbest Properties to Own*. But, for now, the lessons are these:

First lesson: Don't confuse complexity with randomness. Look at a heap of snow, and you see amorphous and undifferentiated white. Examine it much more closely, and you find a collection of exquisitely formed—and highly orderly—snowflake crystals. Listen to Igor Stravinsky's *Rite of Spring* for the very first time, and, chances are, you'll hear nothing more than a collection of violent chords and apparently random rhythm patterns. Exciting, but where's it all headed? Listen two or three times more, and the piece is no less exciting, but it is a whole lot less random and, in fact, begins to appear highly logical. Neither the snow nor the music has changed. Your perception has. You've looked closer. You've gained familiarity.

Most complex structures, systems, and processes appear at first glance random or, at least, impenetrable to the practical understanding.

Given time, effort, and attention, however, many of these entities yield up their order. In the case of business processes—of markets, of production problems, of bottlenecks in negotiation, and so on—a cursory glance is all too often discouraging. We are tempted to throw up our hands, turn the whole thing over to chance, and simply hope for the best. But the more productive approach is to work the problem, looking for the inner order that ties together the superficial confusion.

Second lesson: Look for *useful* order. Confronted with an apparently random, chance-driven, complex, or confusing situation, resist the temptation either to run away or to blindly throw yourself into the fray. Instead, pause to decide just what, exactly, would be *useful* to know in this situation.

In the case of MONOPOLY, you have dice and a forty-square game board—the ingredients, apparently, of randomness or, at the very least, chance. You could turn away from the game board, get up, and walk away, stating proudly: "I prefer games of skill to games of chance." Or you could just start playing, with a comment such as: "Oh, what the hell."

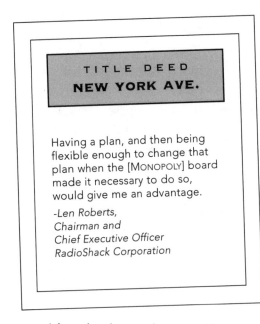

TITLE DEED
NEW YORK AVE.

Having a plan, and then being flexible enough to change that plan when the [MONOPOLY] board made it necessary to do so, would give me an advantage.

-Len Roberts,
*Chairman and
Chief Executive Officer
RadioShack Corporation*

The more productive approach, however, is to decide what would be useful to know—for example, the chance of throwing a seven versus a two, or the chance that an opponent will land on the B & O RAILROAD versus a Green property—then go about discovering how to know it. In MONOPOLY, you can either do the math yourself or pony up a few bucks for *The Monopoly Companion*. In business . . . well, you have to decide what you absolutely need to know and also what would be helpful to know. You don't *absolutely need* to know the chances of landing on a particular property to play MONOPOLY, but the knowledge is certainly helpful, giving you a greater degree of control over play. Likewise, in business, you do not *need* to know what typically concerns customers in the market for the product you sell, but that knowledge is very helpful, increasing your chances of closing sales and of creating customer satisfaction.

Third lesson: Act on what you know. Once you have information, try to put it to work. If you know that customers are concerned about x, y, and z, formulate a good response to these concerns *before* you approach your next customer. Knowledge itself is useless. Application of knowledge is everything.

Chance

I've always been able to make erroneous decisions very quickly.
—Herb Kelleher, founder, Southwest Airlines

IS IT WORTH THE EFFORT?

Defining what you need (or want) to know, then acquiring that knowledge, then applying it to a given situation, can be hard work. In MONOPOLY, you have to ask yourself: Is it harder to do the work, or is it harder to lose? In business, the question can be phrased identically or, if you prefer, this way: Is it harder to do *all* the work and thereby increase the chances that the work will pay off, or is it harder to do only *some* of the work and hope that whatever work you do is not simply wasted, evaporated into the appearance of bad luck and random chaos?

As Benjamin Franklin famously declared, only two things are certain in life: death and taxes.

Actually, death is a lot more certain than taxes. Don't get me wrong. We all pay taxes—sales taxes, transfer taxes, licensing taxes, import taxes (*one* reason why a BMW Z-3 costs more than a Chevy Cavalier), you name it. But let's limit the discussion to income taxes.

INCOME TAX: A SHORT HISTORY

In the United States, taxes on income were introduced as temporary emergency measures to help finance the War of 1812 and, later, the Civil War (1861–1865), but it required an amendment (the Sixteenth) to the Constitution in 1913 to make income tax a permanent fixture of American life. How did our government manage to pull this off? Well, it wasn't the greedy government that forced income tax on the people. It was the people themselves.

For years, working-class and middle-class Americans complained that it was fundamentally unfair for the rich and poor to pay the same taxes. They called instead for a tax pegged to income, which would compel the rich to pay their fair share. Hard to believe it now, but income tax was a very popular proposition early in the twentieth century. It takes a three-quarters majority of the states to ratify a constitutional amendment, which means, roughly, that at least 75 percent of the American voting public *wanted* an income tax.

Would it be hard today to get 8 or even 7 out of every 10 Americans to say they *like* the income tax? Dumb question.

INVESTING IN TAX AVOIDANCE

It is a fact that the rich pay more income tax dollars than the not-so-rich and the poor. However, the rich are almost always more successful at finding ways to reduce their income tax burden than the less wealthy are. Therefore, despite the fact that the rich do pay more tax dollars than the poor, what they pay often represents a lower percentage of their actual income than what most folks pay. This creates the perception that the rich get away with murder or, at the very least, a free ride.

Well, income tax *avoidance*—that is, finding legal ways to reduce one's tax liability—is no free ride. It takes effort, and it takes money. (Note that this is not the same as income tax *evasion*, which is inherently fraudulent and illegal.)

Community Chest

The hardest thing in the world to understand is income tax.

—Attributed to Albert Einstein, American physicist

Rich people create any number of personal corporations to shelter income. They hire high-priced tax attorneys, tax planners, and accountants. Many probably also invest a good deal of energy and effort in worry. Saving dollars from the taxman often requires judgment calls that push the envelope of legality. *Did I push a little too far this time?* Although, we are told, the trend at the IRS has been to reduce the number of audits and investigations, just about everyone knows somebody who's had a run-in with the agency.

And then there are those high-profile stories of celebrities who had major tangles with the taxman. The country-and-western superstar Willie Nelson woke up one morning (he says) to discover that he owed the government the equivalent of the gross national product of a modest Third World nation. A few years ago, Leona Helmsley, the New York hotel magnate celebrated as the "Queen of Mean" because of her allegedly imperious and heartless abuse of her employees, left her mansion for a prison cell due to tax fraud. (It hadn't helped her case any that she was widely reported as having quipped, "I don't pay taxes. Only little people pay taxes.")

Given the volume and complexity of the U.S. tax code, it takes a major business effort to manage one's tax liability—and, even at that, there is often an added cost in anxiety.

IS IT WORTH IT?

Is it worth it?

Once you get beyond the stage of living alone on a single income paid by a single employer who withholds taxes each payday, the answer is *Yes, it's worth it*. It's worthwhile managing your income tax liability, because (as wealthy people know) what matters most is not the money you make, but the money you keep. It is quite possible to be theoretically rich, but still have trouble paying your bills—if your expenses outpace your income. Being wealthy, as opposed to being rich, means that, whatever your income, you live within it *and* have money left over to invest—that is, to make even more money with. The less you hand over to Uncle Sam, the more wealth you preserve. As with any other investment, however, you must decide just how much to risk on tax avoidance. Is it worth the expense and complexity of setting up a corporation? Is the $$$$ penthouse-suite tax accountant really that much better than the $$ storefront one? Is claiming this, that, or the other deduction worth running the risk of an IRS audit?

So is the notion of income tax for the wealthy in reality just a free ride? Hardly. It's hard work. And that brings us back to the MONOPOLY board.

THE "FIXED" TAXES OF MONOPOLY®

There are a number of taxes in MONOPOLY that are fixed—at least in a sense. LUXURY TAX, if you land on it, will cost you $75. Period. If, landing on COMMUNITY CHEST, you draw the "Pay School Tax" card, you'll have to pony up $150, no ifs, ands, or buts about it. If you land on CHANCE, you may draw a card directing you to "Pay Poor Tax of $15." COMMUNITY CHEST and CHANCE also include cards that direct you to make other fixed payments, which aren't called taxes, but which nevertheless take money out of your pocket—for exam-

Community Chest

The Rich aren't like us—they pay less taxes.

—Peter De Vries, American writer

ple, "Doctor's Fee Pay $50" or "You Have Been Elected Chairman of the Board Pay Each Player $50." The COMMUNITY CHEST and CHANCE card stacks also include one card each assessing a tax based on the properties you own: $40 per house, $115 per hotel in COMMUNITY CHEST, and $25 per house and $100 per hotel in CHANCE.

These taxes range from annoying, to significant, to potentially very significant—if, say, you are a big property owner who gets socked with a major per-house, per-hotel assessment. However, it is a bit misleading to call them "fixed" taxes. In contrast to many fixed taxes in the real world, which you can depend on paying with dismal regularity, the fixed taxes in MONOPOLY are relatively rare occurrences. The likelihood of landing on the LUXURY TAX square is about one in ten every time you circuit the board. The likelihood of drawing significant tax (or other payment cards) from COMMUNITY CHEST and CHANCE is even lower per circuit. First, you have to land on a COMMUNITY CHEST or CHANCE square—which, admittedly, is not a rare occurrence—but then you have to be unfortunate enough to draw a tax or payment card. These are far outnumbered by positive cards, cards that pay *you*.

Out of sixteen COMMUNITY CHEST cards, only three will *definitely* cost you money. The GO TO JAIL card will *probably* cost you, although just how much depends on you (see *Lesson 11: On Sitting It Out*). The assessment for street repairs ($40 per house, $115 per hotel) may cost you nothing, if you happen to draw the card when you own no houses or hotels. Every other COMMUNITY CHEST card, eleven of them, *pays* you—ten directly, and one by getting you out of jail for free.

Out of sixteen CHANCE cards, only two *definitely* cost you—and one of these, Pay Poor Tax, demands a mere $15. As with COMMUNITY CHEST, two cards, GO TO JAIL and the Make General Repairs on All Your Property, may or may not cost you.

True to its name, however, CHANCE does contain more cards that may *either* contribute to your income *or* take away from it. Eight cards tell you to go somewhere ("Advance to ILLINOIS AVENUE," for example). This may present you with an opportunity—for instance, to *buy* ILLINOIS AVENUE. Or it may mean nothing much, if you already own ILLINOIS AVENUE. Also, the trip to the property may take you past GO, and thereby put $200 in your pocket. On the other hand, ILLINOIS AVENUE may be part of someone else's major monopoly, and landing on it could cost you as much as $1,100.

Two cards tell you to take a ride on the nearest railroad. This is great if the railroad is unowned—that is, you can buy it or, if the ride takes you around GO, you can collect $200. But if the railroad is owned, then you have to pay the owner "Twice the Rental to which he/she is otherwise entitled."

One card sends you to the nearest utility. If unowned, buy it, if you wish, and if you pass GO, so much the better. If someone else owns the utility, however, you must throw the dice and "pay owner a total ten times the amount thrown."

Nevertheless, none of these cards is a definite (truly "fixed") liability. And, even in the chancy world of CHANCE, four cards are absolute winners, paying *you* $50, $150, and $200 (by taking you to Go); one card gets you out of jail for free.

Chance

Income tax has made more liars out of the American people than golf.

—Will Rogers, American humorist

Think of the LUXURY TAX square and the "bad" COMMUNITY CHEST and CHANCE cards not so much as fixed taxes, but as booby traps, which you may or may not trip over.

INCOME TAX STRATEGIES

INCOME TAX is more flexible than most of the other taxes of MONOPOLY. If you have approximately a 10 percent chance of landing on LUXURY TAX each time you round the board, you have closer to a 12 percent chance of hitting INCOME TAX, just because of its location. However, there may well be many circuits in which INCOME TAX plays no part. It is even possible that you will *never* hit it.

When you do land on this square, you have a decision to make. The fastest and easiest thing to do is to pay $200. But you also have the option of paying 10 percent "of your total worth." This figure includes all your cash, the printed prices of your unmortgaged properties, the mortgaged value of your mortgaged properties, and the cost price of all the buildings that you own.

If you know you're worth $2,000 or more, obviously you should just pay the $200 and get on with your life—or, at least, the game. But a surprising number of players who know they are worth *less* than this amount choose to pay the $200 instead of making the effort to count assets.

"This is supposed to be fun. I don't want to be an accountant," they say. Or: "I don't want to hold up play."

This attitude, of course, costs you money. Why pay $200 when the correct figure is $144? But it can also cost you much more than you realize. By taking the fast and easy way out, you send a message to the other players. You are careless. You are not serious about the game. You are not focused on winning. On the other hand, taking the time to calculate your taxes conveys a lot about your approach to the game. It is serious and determined. Whatever the calculation may save you in immediate dollars, the message sent gives you a significant edge.

Fortunately, deciding on your tax strategy in MONOPOLY does not entail the graver risks that are attached to pushing the income tax envelope in real life. You won't find yourself staring into the cold, dead eyes of an IRS auditor or sharing a cell with a Texas accountant. However, be aware that your decision can go only one way. You must decide whether to pay $200 or 10 percent "before you add up your total worth."

This is one of those MONOPOLY rules often ignored. But it is a rule nonetheless. At the very least, it would seem, the rule calls for skill in estimation or, perhaps, guesstimation. But, if you're playing the game seriously, you shouldn't have to estimate, much less guesstimate. There

Chance

The secret isn't counting the beans, it's growing more beans.

—Roberto Goizueta, former CEO, Coca-Cola Company

is no surer way to get yourself in trouble in business than by remaining blissfully unaware of just what your assets and liabilities are every single day. Serious MONOPOLY *is* serious business and is also *like* serious business. It requires an ongoing, accurate awareness of what you have. Such an awareness is the only sound foundation on which informed decisions can be based, including the decision about whether to pony up $200 or 10 percent.

"This all sounds like work. MONOPOLY is a game. It's supposed to be fun."

Right! It sounds like work because it *is* work. And, right again, it *is* supposed to be fun. That is the great, delicious secret of MONOPOLY. It models business, and in the MONOPOLY model of business, work is what it should be. Fun. Now, get to work.

"There's no such thing as a free lunch," the old saying goes. Hundreds of thousands, maybe even millions, of MONOPOLY players—misguided MONOPOLY players, that is—might argue with this.

That's because they wrongly believe that all luxury taxes and one-time "fines" and other random charges should get placed in a pile—the "kitty"—and reserved for the next lucky stiff who happens to land on the corner opposite GO.

"Hey, land on FREE PARKING, and you get whatever's in the kitty. That's how we've always played it!"

THE UNANSWERED QUESTION

Community Chest

We all know that if we stand still, we go backwards. You have to be willing to make decisions and take risks.

—*Sanford I Weill, CEO, Citigroup*

You know those deep, maybe ultimately unanswerable, cosmic questions that folks sometimes like to ask, such as, *Do neutrinos really account for most of the matter in the universe?* or *Why is the water always colder out of the bathroom tap?* Well, when it comes to MONOPOLY, there's an eually obscure question that fits right in: *Whose idea was it to make a giant piñata out of the FREE PARKING space?*

Not only do the rules make no mention of a "kitty" into which all MONOPOLY fines, fees, and taxes are put, to be collected by the lucky stiff who lands on FREE PARKING, the rules explicitly bar this practice: "A player landing on this place does not receive any money, property or reward of any kind. This is just a 'free' resting place."

The rules notwithstanding, many players insist on the FREE PARKING kitty.

Chance

The man who goes the furthest is generally the one who is willing to do and dare.

—Dale Carnegie, author of How to Win Friends and Influence People

A BAD IDEA

Apart from its being unsanctioned, if not expressly disapproved, such a jackpot trivializes the game. Certainly, it does violence to MONOPOLY as a model of business life. True, in real life, some people do win big playing the lottery, but the chances of that in any one lifetime are too slim to be accurately modeled in a three-hour game. The fact is that the FREE PARKING jackpot is bogus and should be resolutely abandoned and avoided.

That said, what's left?

Chance The moment you let avoiding failure become your motivator, you're down the path of inactivity.

—Roberto Goizueta, former CEO, Coca-Cola Company

No free lunch, but, as the rules put it, "a 'free' resting place." Nothing too bad about that—but nothing good, either. In fact, resting is not a good idea in MONOPOLY. Ending a turn in FREE PARKING costs you nothing out of your pocket, it is true, but it does cost you whatever opportunity that turn might otherwise have represented.

THE PERIL OF PASSIVITY

If there *is* value to FREE PARKING, it is as an object lesson in the price of passivity. Do you feel safe on FREE PARKING? ("At least I didn't land on Joe's hotel-infested KENTUCKY AVENUE.") You shouldn't; you should feel anxious. What you consider safety is actually a missed opportunity.

LOCKED UP IS LOCKED DOWN

With FREE PARKING, you're in, then out on the very next turn. Going to jail is a less certain proposition.

You get sent to jail "(1) when your token lands on the space marked GO TO JAIL; (2) when you draw a card marked GO TO JAIL; or (3) when you throw doubles three times in succession." Given all these punishable "crimes," the odds are that, in any given game, you will go to jail—and probably more than once.

> **Community Chest**
>
> The greatest danger is in standing still.
> —Andrew S. Grove, chairman, Intel Corporation

You may get out of jail via any of four routes: by "(1) throwing doubles on any of your next three turns . . . , (2) using your GET OUT OF JAIL FREE card, if you have one; (3) purchasing the GET OUT OF JAIL FREE card from another player and playing it; (4) paying a fine of $50 . . ." The catch to option 4 is that you must pay the fine *before* rolling the dice; that is, you can't roll in the hope of doubles, then, failing doubles, pony up the

$50. It's either/or: roll and hope, or just pay up—then get on with game.

A surprising number of players prefer to rot in jail for as many as two turns in the vain hope of rolling doubles and thereby saving $50. Some people just can't pass up a bargain, but this kind of sweat equity could drive you broke. If ending just one turn in the neutrality of FREE PARKING is not a good thing, how much worse to let the world pass you by in jail through maybe *two* turns. (At least it won't be three, because if you fail to roll doubles on your third try, you *must* pay the $50, then immediately move the number of spaces you've rolled.)

BAD BARGAIN, GOOD BARGAIN

Hoping to roll doubles in lieu of immediately paying the fine is a bad gamble and a false economy. Fifty bucks is a small price to pay to avoid losing opportunities.

By the way, don't be *too* hasty about plunking down your $50. If another player has a GET OUT OF JAIL FREE card and is willing to part with it for less than $50, buy it and play it. However, it should be noted that good players seldom sell this card. It's too valuable as insurance against "opportunity loss."

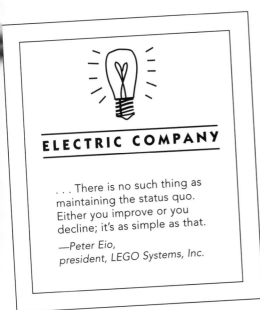

ELECTRIC COMPANY

. . . There is no such thing as maintaining the status quo. Either you improve or you decline; it's as simple as that.

—Peter Eio,
president, LEGO Systems, Inc.

LISTEN TO THE LESSON

Much of what has just been said will doubtless fall on deaf ears. For as many players as there are willing to lose a couple of turns rather than part with $50, even more actually believe jail provides the same safe haven as FREE PARKING supposedly does. This point of view is especially common late in the game, among players short of cash and low on properties. In jail, they feel, they won't lose any money—and it is possible, just possible, that one of the other players will, in the meantime, meet with disaster.

In truth, this point of view makes no sense. While it is true that you won't land on somebody else's BOARDWALK while sitting in jail, neither will you enjoy the opportunity to do anything positive. Even worse, you cannot collect rents while in jail, so any properties you own are idled. As for the other guy's disasters, well, they're just as likely to occur whether or not you happen to be locked up.

> ### Community Chest
>
> The only time you don't fail is the last time you try something, and it works.
>
> —Charles Franklin Kettering, American businessman and engineer

Listen, here's the lesson to take away: Inaction confers the illusion of safety. That is the most it can do for you. The point of MONOPOLY, as of any life lived in business, is to play. Fifty dollars is one of the cheapest tickets in town, whereas the price of missed opportunity is far more than you can afford.

Most of us know people who've worked hard at some profession or some business idea, developed it, made a success of it, and put money in the bank. You look at the career of such a person, and the root and course of her success is obvious: hard work and focused work. But then most of us also know people who operate, well, rather more deviously. They aren't necessarily dishonest or lazy or dishonorable. They just seem naturally to "know all the angles" and to play those angles very, very well. They're the ones who set up various corporations, tax shelters, holding companies, you name it. We say of these folks that they don't work *hard*, they work *smart*.

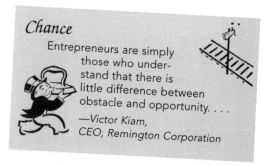

Chance

Entrepreneurs are simply those who understand that there is little difference between obstacle and opportunity. . . .
—*Victor Kiam*,
CEO, Remington Corporation

THE SIMPLE AND THE DEVIOUS

MONOPOLY can be played—and often won—very simply. Just buy everything in sight. It is possible that you'll go broke, but it is also possible that you'll win. A recklessly aggressive player has a better chance of winning than a cautiously conservative player. In MONOPOLY, investors do much better than savers—though both may lose in the end.

MONOPOLY can by played simply, but it can also be played—and won—deviously. Here's how.

ANATOMY OF A HOUSING SHORTAGE

One of the slickest and yet least exploited "angles" in MONOPOLY is the strategy of the housing shortage.

First, take a fresh look at the rules: "The Bank never 'goes broke.' If the Bank runs out of money, the Banker may issue as much more as may be needed by writing on any ordinary paper."

So much for trying to create a money shortage. However, the bank also holds the houses and hotels. What happens when you run out of either of these?

Let's refer to the rules: "BUILDING SHORTAGES . . . When the Bank has no houses to sell, players wishing to build must wait for some player to return or sell his/her houses to the Bank before building. If there is a limited number of houses and hotels available and two or more players wish to buy more than the Bank has, the houses or hotels must be sold at auction to the highest bidder."

Surprisingly few players give this strategically important rule much thought. Think about it now. What are houses and hotels? Little green and red plastic toys? Yes, and no. What they are in the world of the game is opportunity. Each house, each hotel, is an opportunity to make another player pay you. Like most opportunities, these are limited in quantity. There are 32 houses and 12 hotels. There are 22 color properties. To put four houses on each would require 88 houses. There are only 32 in the game. To put one hotel on each would require 22 hotels. The bank's got 12.

Chance

Don't buy hotels. If possible, buy only houses. Tie them up and create a housing shortage.

—Greg Jacobs, 1983 MONOPOLY World Champion

CREATING DEFEAT

As we'll learn in *Lesson 16: The Real Object of the Game*, the winner of MONOPOLY is not the player with the greatest assets, but the player who does not go bankrupt. In effect, the real object of the game is not necessarily to "win," but to make everyone else lose.

Community Chest

That is the trouble with prosperity— it hides the defects of a business.
—Harvey Firestone, founder, Firestone Tire and Rubber

You make the others lose by costing them money—or by depriving them of opportunity. One of the most influential means of accomplishing the latter is by creating a housing shortage.

AN ENDGAME STRATEGY

The best time to create a housing shortage is during the endgame, the point of play in which there are few if any properties left to buy and virtually no chance of acquiring any new monopolies. Now all players are focused on—or, at least, should be focused on—developing the monopolies they have.

Most players at this stage will blithely trade in houses for hotels. In the endgame, this is typically a mistake. By returning houses to the bank, you provide opportunity to another player to develop a more potent monopoly. Be aware of how many houses are left in the bank. If the supply is dwindling, let it dwindle. Don't take the knee-jerk route of automatically trading up to a hotel. Remember, any hotels sitting in the bank are useless if a player doesn't have four houses on a given property to trade. Houses are the key. Know when to create a housing shortage.

THE BEST DEFENSE . . .

You create a housing shortage not just by refraining from upgrading to hotels, but also by buying as many houses as possible. This is where those low-rent properties, the deep purples and the light blues, come in handy. If you own a low-rent monopoly, build it up with houses. It won't cost you much to drain the bank's supply of them by planting four on each of the deep purples or light blues. This is both a good offensive move and a sound defensive one. An opponent who owns a high-priced monopoly can't do too much damage with it if you've sucked up all the houses.

Nor does creating a housing shortage have to be an all-or-nothing proposition. You may not be able to empty the bank of houses, but you can probably deplete it, so that your orange-owning opponent can put only one house on each of those expensive properties instead of four. This means that landing on NEW YORK AVENUE will be a costly annoyance for you instead of a financial disaster, and it also means that your opponent will never be able to realize the full potential of his investment. Serves him right.

KNOWING THE MARKET, CONTROLLING THE MARKET

The availability of housing is all about the market. It is very useful to know the market: How many houses are available? It is even more use-

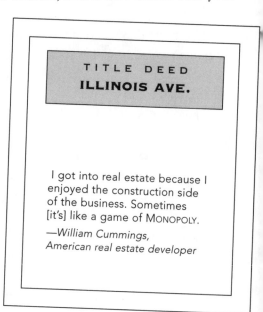

TITLE DEED
ILLINOIS AVE.

I got into real estate because I enjoyed the construction side of the business. Sometimes [it's] like a game of MONOPOLY.

—William Cummings,
American real estate developer

ful to gain some measure of control over the market by creating a housing shortage, especially during the endgame.

At bottom, just about all competitive businesses are about markets. With luck, you may be able to survive in a business without knowing much about some of these markets, but you will surely be at a disadvantage. You may conduct your business by picturing yourself as a cork bobbing helplessly on the waves of the market. You can stay afloat, but where you'll wind up is anyone's guess.

PENNSYLVANIA R.R.

Some people think that Japan's success is due to cartels and collaboration. It is not. It has many fiercely competitive local rivals.

—Michael Porter, American economic strategist

Or you may try to control that market or some sector of the market. To the degree that you can purposefully influence the market, your success is likely to increase.

Achieving such control starts with knowledge, with learning everything you can about the markets that affect your business. From here, it's a question of figuring out the angles. Sometimes you must look beyond the obvious and reflexive. As the by-now shopworn phrase has it, you must think outside the box.

Everyone knows the object of building on those MONOPOLY monopolies is to get hotels. Maybe it's time to turn away from what *everyone knows*. Work the angle others don't see. Hold on to your four houses instead, save a little extra money that you'd have spent on hotels, and keep your opponents' opportunities to a minimum.

The darkest blindness in business is seeing only how a move you make affects you. Look beyond yourself. How does your move affect others? What impact does it have on the environment in which your business and the businesses of others exist? That is, how does your move i mpact the market?

In MONOPOLY, the player who knows when and how to create a housing shortage, to choke off the opportunity available to others while maximizing his own, is the player whose eyes are wide open and who sees the farthest in all directions.

"What business are you in?"

It's a common enough question, certainly. But can you answer it? The fact is that most people get it wrong, at least off the top of their head.

They answer something like this: "I sell shoes," or "I'm in the candy business," or "I'm in real estate," or "I'm a plumber," or something else, moving right on down the 23 major groups of the United States Bureau of Labor Statistics *Standard Occupational Classification* system.

And they answer wrong.

Chance

On negotiation: Anxiety will disappear when you recognize that both sides can have their needs met.

—Ed Brodow, American author and consultant

WHAT BUSINESS ARE YOU IN?

"What business are you in?"

You're in the people business. It doesn't matter what you do, what you make, what you sell—you can't do, make, or sell anything without doing business with people. These people include customers, prospective customers, former customers, employees, colleagues, consultants, bosses, investors, vendors, government officials, competitors, and creditors, among others. To get at the business you *think* you're in, you have to succeed at the business you're *certainly* in: people.

"What game are you playing?"

"MONOPOLY, of course."

"How do you play it?"

"Well, you roll dice, and you move around the board, and you buy properties from the bank, and you pay and collect rent, and. . . ."

Let's stop right here. *What* game are you playing?

"I'm not playing a game. I'm playing people."

Correct.

Community Chest

My father said: You must never try to make all the money that's in a deal. Let the other fellow make some money too.

—J. Paul Getty, American oil magnate

Make no mistake. You are not playing the bank, you are not playing the board, you are not playing the dice. You are playing people. That is something no winning MONOPOLY player can afford to forget. But it is not something anyone is likely to remind you of. The official rules say almost nothing about it, and players often seem to forget about it as well.

RULES OF TRADE

In Part II, we'll discuss the myriad angles of playing people, but one of the most important aspects we can discuss right here and right now.

You won't find much about trading in the official rules of MONOPOLY. However, you will find that trading is not only permitted, but it is also an important part of sound MONOPOLY strategy.

First, note that there are limits to what you can trade:
• You cannot trade houses and hotels. If you want to trade a property that has houses or hotels on it, you must first sell these back to the bank—at half price. (So be sure to figure *that* into your cost of doing business.)
• You cannot trade your turn.
• You cannot trade a pledge of immunity from paying rent on a certain property.
• You cannot trade a guarantee that you won't build houses on a given property.
• You cannot trade a loan.

What you *can* trade are the following:
• Title deeds
• Cash
• GET OUT OF JAIL FREE cards

For instance, you can trade your PACIFIC AVENUE for Sam's ILLINOIS AVENUE. You can trade your READING RAILROAD and WATER WORKS for Ed's PARK PLACE. You can pay Sam, in cash, for VENTNOR AVENUE, settling on whatever price is mutually agreeable. You can sell your GET OUT OF JAIL FREE card to Mary, or you might use it to sweeten a deal you want to make, such as: "Look, I'll throw in a GET OUT OF JAIL FREE card. . . ." (A word to the wise: Don't part with a GET OUT OF JAIL FREE card for cash. Keep it reserved as what the folks in New Orleans call *lagniappe*, that little something extra that gets a reluctant dealer off the dime.)

Chance When one loses in a particular competitive negotiation, one's chances of winning the next negotiation are frequently diminished.
—Theodore Zeldin, Israeli thinker and historian

When can you make a trade?

The rules are very liberal in this regard. You may make a deal with another player during your turn, either before you roll the dice or afterward, and you may even make a deal between the turns of other players. In jail? So what? Keep on trading.

WHY DO IT?

How important is trading?

Consider this: Trading is the only way to raise money on demand without mortgaging a property or selling hotels and houses back to the Bank. If you need money *now*, trading may well be your best option. Otherwise, you have to wait for a lucky COMMUNITY CHEST or CHANCE card, another player to land on one of your properties, or a trip past GO.

Trading is also a way of acquiring properties you really want but others got to first. At mid game, a good trade may revive a lost opportunity to build a monopoly. Say you own MARVIN GARDENS, Sam owns VENTNOR AVENUE, and ATLANTIC AVENUE's still in the bank. Now is the time to try to trade or buy VENTNOR AVENUE—*before* you've acquired ATLANTIC AVENUE. If you hold two yellow properties, Sam is not very likely to sell you the third—at least not at anything like a realistic price, unless he's in very deep trouble. However, if one property is still up for grabs, Sam may well be in a mood to deal.

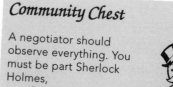

Community Chest

A negotiator should observe everything. You must be part Sherlock Holmes, part Sigmund Freud.
—Victor Kiam CEO, Remington Corporation

Trading is also a good tactic for blocking another player. Mary owns PENNSYLVANIA AVENUE and NORTH CAROLINA AVENUE. Sam owns PACIFIC AVENUE. He's on the verge of bankruptcy. Suspecting he might, in desperation, offer Mary the very property she needs to complete her monopoly, you decide to move proactively and make him an offer. Your object is to keep PACIFIC AVENUE out of Mary's hands.

There is a risk here, of course, in that your offer may start a bidding war. Mary may decide that it's worth getting PACIFIC AVENUE at practically any price. Not only would this give Mary a valuable monopoly, it would supply Sam with a transfusion of cash that could get him back into the game—and, remember, the real object of MONOPOLY is not so much to win as it is to make others lose, to drive them out of the game.

As is apparent from these two scenarios, player-to-player trading opens the game up to increased opportunity as well as increased risk. But if *you* don't take the risk, another player will take the opportunity.

SELL VALUE

You enter into a trade because you believe it will benefit you. That much is obvious. However, don't let yourself be hemmed in by this obvious, but narrow, perspective.

Too many traders view themselves not as traders but as bargain hunters, people who want to get something for next to nothing. Limiting yourself to this kind of deal means that a lot of opportunities will pass you by. The essence of trading is an exchange of value for value, something you want for something the other person wants.

Chance

When money is at stake, never be the first to mention sums.
—*Sheikh Ahmed Zaki Yamani, Saudi politician and businessman*

Your best shot at making a good trade is to sell value. The rookie salesman makes the mistake of selling price rather than value: "This vacuum cleaner is a real bargain. No one sells it for less." True, most people want to get the lowest price. But the lowest price of all is $0—no sale—and pushing your customer in that direction will give *you* no benefit at all.

What people want even more than the lowest price is the best value. The customer drooling in the new car showroom certainly does not want to pay top dollar, but neither does he want to walk away from the showroom. A good salesperson will close the deal by persuading the customer that he is getting good value for the money he parts with.

Approach the other player not in the spirit of forcing him into a bad bargain, but of giving him good value. Put the emphasis on what *he* is getting from you, not what you are getting from him.

Think about it: The car salesman doesn't entice you by saying, "Look, you just give me $25,000. I'll get a commission and pay my mortgage this month. And, uh, oh yeah, you get this car over here." Instead, he keeps the focus on the value the customer is acquiring. He demonstrates the car. He asks questions about what the customer needs. He shows how this particular car satisfies those needs. He never once mentions the mortgage he has to pay—even though this is immeasurably more important to him than whether the car has cup holders in the front as well as the back.

"Sam, it's obvious you need cash to stay in the game. That's what I'm offering you."

And that is where you stop. There is no need to explain to Sam what *you* are getting out of the deal: Ventnor Avenue and a shot at a monopoly. Keep the focus on the benefit to Sam. Beyond this, don't threaten or cajole or plead. He may notice that you already hold Marvin Gardens and will probably assume that you will soon be going for the monopoly if you can get Atlantic Avenue. But you didn't say that. You didn't even imply it. (Or, at least, you shouldn't have.)

NAME NO PRICE

Offer value, but name no price. In any negotiation, the first person to set a figure is always in the weaker position. Avoid saying, "Sam, I'll give you $300 for VENTNOR AVENUE." Instead, start with, "Sam, what do you want for VENTNOR AVENUE?" Then work down from the figure he gives you. Once you get Sam to name his price, he can't reasonably ask for more. If the price is going to go anywhere, it's down.

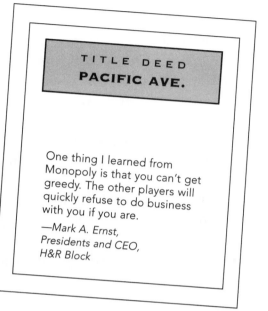

TITLE DEED
PACIFIC AVE.

One thing I learned from Monopoly is that you can't get greedy. The other players will quickly refuse to do business with you if you are.
—Mark A. Ernst, Presidents and CEO, H&R Block

ASK QUESTIONS

Want to kill a negotiation? Focus on your needs. Want to keep a negotiation alive? Focus on the other person's needs.

Ask questions: "Sam, what do you want for VENTNOR AVENUE?" Or: "Sam, you're cash poor. Do you *want* to stay in the game?" Or: "Sam, how long do you think you can last with that monopoly of yours mortgaged?"

Get the other person to focus on what he needs and how what you offer will satisfy that need.

BARGAINING BOOT CAMP

In making a trade, your job is to persuade your trading partner that you are, indeed, offering value. In business this can be challenging; however, you are often aided by the conventions of commerce—what you and the other person understand, for example, by the concept of customer and seller. It is *relatively* easy for an automobile salesman to persuade a customer to part with money in exchange for a car. The customer wants to drive. The customer needs a car. The customer understands that he has to pay for this product he both wants and needs.

Even though you're playing with MONOPOLY money, it may be more difficult to persuade the person sitting across the game board that the deal you want to make is beneficial to him. After all, you are not vendor and customer, but opponent and opponent.

This is the core challenge of making trades in MONOPOLY, and if you can make a good deal in MONOPOLY, in which the climate is both fun yet inherently hostile, you can make a good deal in the real world of business. Piece of cake.

In MONOPOLY, auctions are not optional. They are the rule. You land on a property and, "If you do not wish to buy the property," the official rules say, "the Banker sells it at auction to the highest bidder." Nothing voluntary here. Each piece of unbought property *must* be put up for auction.

This doesn't mean that everyone, or even anyone, has to bid on every property that comes up for auction. But as we've learned already, winners more often than not are very aggressive purchasers of property. Odds are, if you and your opponents are playing to win, there will be at least one bid every time a property lands on the auction block.

EVERYONE IN

Who can bid?

Anyone. And that includes the person who chose not to buy the property when he landed on it.

What is the order of the bidding?

Absolutely none. It's a free for all. Anyone can bid in any order, provided that each bid is higher than the previous one.

Where does the bidding start?

It starts anywhere. It can start at a dollar. There is no "reserve," no minimum bid. Although the Banker conducts the auction, she has no authority to set a minimum or to demand minimum increments. This notwithstanding, players should bear in mind that starting at one dollar and increasing the bid dollar by dollar is almost certain to result in a very tedious exchange that significantly slows play. If you want the property, start at a low but realistic figure, then bid up by reasonable increments, say five or ten dollars. In general, as we'll discuss in just a moment, it *is* best to start below the property's mortgaged value; that is, start the bidding at less than one-half the printed price.

The Banker, by the way, conducts the auction, but, as a player, may also participate in the bidding. This puts a special burden on the Banker to behave in a manner that is both courteous and fair. When a high bid seems to have been reached, the Banker must give fair warning. Something traditional will work quite adequately: "I have $80. Do I hear more? Going once at $80. *[Take a beat.]* Going twice. *[Another beat.]* Gone! Sold to Mary for $80."

OBJECT OF AN AUCTION

In the world beyond the game board, many people attend auctions in the hope of getting a spectacular bargain. Sometimes they do. Often, however, the excitement of the auction drives bids well above the bargain range.

Chance

I buy when other people are selling.
—J. Paul Getty, American oil magnate

Young children typically love auctions.

"Did we win?" they ask in great excitement.

The adult patiently explains that you don't really "win" an auction. You do have to *pay* for what you get.

"Yes, but did we *win?*"

Chance

When nobody wants something, that creates an opportunity.
—Carl C. Icahn, American financier

The child's view of the auction is not very different from the way many of us adults view the event. Many of us see an auction as a contest or competition, and, holding this view, it is easy to lose sight of the fact that acquisition is not the sole object of the auction. The idea is to get what you want without paying too much. In an auction, "victory at any price" is, by definition, no victory. The object is to achieve victory at a good price—that is, to gain value, not lose it.

AUCTION A LA MONOPOLY®

This said, MONOPOLY auctions do not typically result in players paying outrageous prices for properties. Usually, the sale price is below the printed price for the property. This is because most players buy most of the properties they land on when they land on them. Properties tend to go up for auction only under one of two circumstances:

1. The property has little hope of being developed into a monopoly. For example, you land on VIRGINIA AVENUE. Joe already owns STATES AVENUE, and Mary owns ST. CHARLES PLACE. You decide not to buy. (Of course, if Joe owned both STATES AVENUE and ST. CHARLES PLACE, you'd almost certainly do well to snap up VIRGINIA AVENUE to prevent Joe from acquiring a monopoly.)

2. The player who lands on the property has little or no money and can't afford the parcel.

Bear in mind that it is always worth acquiring a property—*any* property—for less than its mortgaged value. You can always convert the property into cash, and with positive cashflow, too.

Should you ever bid *more* than the property's printed price?

Let's consider this apparent test of logic. . . .

FORGET PRICE, EMBRACE VALUE

There is nothing sacred about price. The important issue is value. If you own VIRGINIA and STATES AVENUES, and ST. CHARLES PLACE comes up for auction, this property represents a high value even if you have to pay much more than the $140 printed price. By the same token, it is worth paying a high price to block another player who owns two of the three light purples in order to deprive him of a monopoly. In this latter case, you can recoup some of your cash outlay, if necessary, by immediately mortgaging the property.

The great lesson of an auction is not getting a steal, buying something on the cheap, or "winning" against other bidders. No. The take-away lesson of the auction is that your goal is to get value.

Price is a number. It is fixed, absolute, and more or less arbitrary. Value, in contrast, is a relative matter, and it is never arbitrary. Value is the ratio of cost versus benefit at a given time and

Community Chest

A business . . . has to be dynamic. The world around us changes all the time and there can be no holy cows.

—*Nicola Horlick, British fund manager*

within a given set of circumstances. In some circumstances, paying $200 for ST. CHARLES PLACE—where the printed price is $140—would be outrageous, foolish, and a terrible value. But at a certain time and within the appropriate set of circumstances, as much as $500 would represent an outstanding value.

MONOPOLY, like business—as we have already said more than once—is dynamic. Each turn is played within a changing framework of relationships, opportunities, and liabilities. A static approach to any dynamic system, whether that system is the game of business or the

Community Chest

On auctions: It's not about ego or talent. It's simply about raising your hand for the next bid. They won. We lost. Next.

—*Barry Diller, American media mogul*

business of MONOPOLY, is bound to fail sooner or later. Thinking in terms of price—whether a bargain or "victory at any cost"—is thinking in static terms. Winning MONOPOLY, as with succeeding in business, demands the dynamic approach embodied in the concept of value, which weighs cost against benefit in the context of time and circumstance. This is not the easy way out, but it really is the only way in—in and onward.

In the real world, bankruptcy is not a dirty word. Nor is it necessarily the end of a business; in fact, modern bankruptcy laws exists largely to give businesses and individuals the financial breathing space they need to scratch out a fresh start.

WHEN BANKRUPTCY WAS REALLY BAD

Things weren't always so benevolent and understanding. That strange word, *bankruptcy*, has its origin in renaissance Italy. Back then, a *banca* was a moneychanger's table. The word *rotta* is the past participle of *rompere*, to break. When a moneychanger made enough bad deals to drain him of funds, he kicked over his bench, breaking the *banca*. This meant that he was through, washed up, his moneychanging days over (at least for a while).

Chance

Capitalism without bankruptcy is like Christianity without hell.

—Frank Borman,
American astronaut and
business executive

Even more recently, up through much of the twentieth century, bankruptcy was a disgrace that drove many people permanently out of business at best and, at worst, drove not a few to suicide.

Yet nowadays, despite occasional congressional moves to "tighten up" bankruptcy laws or "close bankruptcy loopholes," people and businesses routinely survive bankruptcy, often more than a few times.

As far as bankruptcy is concerned, MONOPOLY is much more like the old days than modern times. In MONOPOLY, when you go broke, you kick over the bench—and bow out of the game. You're through. You're done. You lose.

In MONOPOLY, "you are declared bankrupt if you owe more than you can pay either to another player or to the Bank." It's that simple, and it's that absolute. You lose everything.

THE FOLLY OF SAFETY

How do you avoid bankruptcy?

In real life, life beyond the game board, the typical answers are something like "Play it safe," "Be conservative," "Put something away for a rainy day," or "Don't take chances." In real life, pursuing a course in the spirit of such mild advice may well save you from bankruptcy, but it is not likely to bring you wealth. The prospect of reward is always accompanied by the necessity of risk.

Chance   I detest bankruptcy. To me it signifies failure—personal failure, corporate failure.

—George Steinbrenner, owner, New York Yankees

MONOPOLY creates a more intense and dramatic situation than real life. As in real life, playing it safe will almost certainly prevent you from becoming wealthy. Unlike real life, however, holding to the safe path will not keep you from going bankrupt. Aggressive play and risk taking may hurl you headlong into bankruptcy, it is true. But players who fail to be aggressive, who fail to take risks, are all but certain to fall victim to their opponents. In MONOPOLY, it is eat or be eaten. Shrink from risk, and you are virtually assured of going bankrupt, and maybe sooner than you think.

Community Chest

Failing is good as long as it doesn't become a habit.

—Michael Eisner, chairman and CEO, Disney Corporation

PLAYING OFFENSE

So, how do you avoid bankruptcy in MONOPOLY?

That question implies that you need to take a defensive position—that is, you are trying to avoid a *possible* occurrence. But most of the time, a staunchly defensive philosophy proves to be too conservative.

The best defense, it turns out, is a good offense. Play aggressively. Acquire property. Invest in creating an environment that will prove costly to everyone else in the game. MONOPOLY models the foundation assumption of economics: the principle of scarcity. Every opportunity you act on is an opportunity that is thereby denied to another player.

THE ALAMO DEFENSE

Yet aggressive play does not guarantee that you will avoid bankruptcy and, therefore, win. It is quite possible to overspend yourself. It is certainly possible that your monopolies just won't gel fast enough. It is distressingly possible that your opponents will, somehow, time after time, avoid landing on your best monopolies, while you, in contrast, keep stumbling onto theirs. Stuff happens.

In short, despite your good offense, you might find yourself on the verge of kicking over the bench.

When this happens, it's time for the Alamo defense: desperate but deft moves to raise cash and buy time in the hope that your monopolies will begin to pay off, bail you out, and raise you back up on your feet again. As long as you're in the game, you have a chance, and the object of the Alamo defense is to stay in the game.

Your first resort in this last-resort Alamo strategy is to mortgage any single properties you may own. After you mortgage single properties, mortgage those colors you have two of. Then mortgage any single utilities you have, and then any railroads. Finally, as a last resort, start mortgaging your monopolies.

Remember, the colored properties closest to GO have the least chance of being landed on. Therefore, mortgage these first.

In addition to mortgaging properties, look for opportunities to make deals with other players. You cannot borrow money from others, but you can sell them property. Except in the most desperate of circumstances, do not sell another player the very property she needs to complete a monopoly. Everything else, however, is fair game.

Chance

Failing is a learning experience. It can be a gravestone or a stepping stone.

—Bud Hadfield, founder, Kwik Kopy

THE ALAMO OPTION

You may not want to play the Alamo defense until you become desperate. So until then, you may choose to kick it down a notch and play the Alamo *option*.

Consider mortgaging properties whenever you have an opportunity to buy something that will help you win—a monopoly, for sure, but also houses and more houses. As the game nears the end, push the envelope.

Buy more aggressively than ever, even if this means mortgaging heavily, because the pool of available properties and the bank's supply of houses is shrinking fast.

Can such aggressive play bring disaster? Absolutely. But it can also turn a game around for you, and it is a worthwhile strategy if you find yourself lagging substantially behind another player.

The main purpose of the Alamo defense is to buy time. The only thing better than buying time is buying opportunity. If you mortgage and trade aggressively *before* you're down to your last few dollars, it is opportunity that you'll be bidding for, and opportunity, in turn, does not merely *buy* time, it *creates* time.

As a plot device in science fiction, it's become pretty standard: Strange things start happening. Reality is eerily altered. The cause? It's usually revealed about 20 minutes into the movie or 30 pages into the novel. The hero discovers—gasp!—a *parallel universe*.

That parallel universe, an alternate reality, does not cancel out or replace the familiar universe, but, once it's found, it can be manipulated to complement, augment, and, as it were, *supercharge* ordinary reality. Misused, however, it brings cosmic disaster. Either way, it's a whole new set of rules, parallel with the familiar and commonly accepted ones. In skilled hands, the secret rules are a source of positive power; in the hands of the uninformed and unaware, they are a cause of defeat and destruction.

We look now at the unwritten rules of MONOPOLY, knowledge of which will help you win—win this game, as well as the bigger games of decision making and deal making in the world of business that MONOPOLY models.

THE *REAL* OBJECT OF THE GAME

In 1984, entrepreneur Mark H. McCormack published what became a sensation as *the* anti-rule book of business: *What They Don't Teach You at Harvard Business School*. In its essentials, the world of business in 1984 was not all that different from what it is today. Among many other things, that world was divided into two opposite camps: In Camp A, there were the people who thought a Harvard MBA—or its equivalent—virtually guaranteed success. There were rules in business, and if you learned the rules better than just about anyone else, you could play the game better than just about anyone else. In Camp B were those who believed success crowned not the rule-book-reading plodders, but the mavericks, the people who set out purposely to break the rules.

McCormack introduced a third point of view. The question he asked was not whether to master and obey the rules or ignore and break the rules, but *What* are *the rules*? The *real* rules. The only rules that really, finally matter—the rules (he said) they don't teach you at Harvard Business School.

NEAT GAME, MESSY LIFE

It takes at least two years of graduate work to earn a Harvard MBA. In contrast, the rules of MONOPOLY fit on a folded-paper insert and can be read in a matter of minutes. As two years in graduate school is no guarantee of a winning career, so ten minutes inside a MONOPOLY box does not ensure victory in the game. After all, there are rules, and then there are *your* rules.

At the root of the pleasure of most games is the way in which they mirror and model life. For many kids, MONOPOLY is an introduction to such real-life activities as handling money, making money, saving money, spending money, making deals, and even coping with financial crisis and hardship. Yet what makes any game mostly more fun than real life is the single biggest difference between gaming and living. A game enfolds us in a warm, secure cocoon of unambiguous and unbreakable rules. Life offers no such thing. Oh, there are plenty of rules, instructions, regulations, stipulations, warnings, mandates, and laws, but their meaning isn't always clear, and their effect is rarely certain.

Open a factory-fresh MONOPOLY set. Slice through the shrink wrap. Lift off the box top. Feel the suck of the vacuum as the top and bottom reluctantly separate. Look at the cellophane-wrapped currency, the CHANCE and COMMUNITY CHEST cards, the houses and hotels, the player tokens, the dice, the folded board, each nestled in its own section of the molded plastic tray. Take a deep breath and inhale the crisp scent of freshly printed play money.

Chance

It is not enough to succeed. Others must fail.

—Attributed to Gore Vidal, American author

Who hasn't lingered, hesitated just a bit, in the act of opening a new MONOPOLY set? There is— what can you call it?—a certain poignancy in realizing that the money, the cards, the pieces will never be this clean, crisp, and neat—this *promising*—again.

Then there is real life. It is never this clean, crisp, neat, or promising. It is, from the very beginning, messy, and we spend our years looking for ways to sort it out. Some seek a set of rules and try to follow them. Some go out of their way to break whatever rules they find. And others discover the rules that are rarely taught and that are little known. There are no guarantees, of course, but it is the people in this third category who generally enjoy disproportionate success.

OF THE FIRST RULE

Lift off the MONOPOLY box top, pull out the rules page, and read the first rule. Under the heading "OBJECT," we read: "The object of the game is to become the wealthiest player through buying, renting and selling property."

What could be clearer?

And what could be more wrong?

Okay. You've just lifted the top off the box. Not only have you yet to begin playing, you've barely finished reading the first rule. But it is at this stage that you need to think through to the very end of the game.

Chance

TOOT

I don't meet competition. I crush it.
—Charles Revson,
founder, Revlon, Inc.

What is the most desirable situation when play is over? Is it to be the "wealthiest player"? That's what the official rules say. But think *through* the official rules, and what you must conclude is that the most desirable situation at the end of the game is to be the winner, and, in MONOPOLY, the winner is not just the *wealthiest* person in the game, but the *only* person left in the game. The object, therefore, is "to become the *only* player."

What happened to everybody else?

They lost, and if you played the game well, they lost because you made them lose. How? "Through buying, renting and selling property," just as the rule says. That this made you the "wealthiest player" is, however, irrelevant. The only relevant effect of your buying, renting and selling property is that it made the others poor, drove them, in fact, into bankruptcy and out of the game.

So here is *your* rule #1. Under the heading "OBJECT": "The object of the game is to buy, rent and sell property with sufficiently focused and ruthless skill to bankrupt the other players and thereby force them out of the game."

CAN YOU DEAL WITH IT?

Games have winners and losers. A game in which everyone wins is no game at all. It may be an activity, but it's not much fun—although it may be marginally more enjoyable than a game in which everyone loses.

Except for the most politically correct among us, we have little trouble accepting a game whose object is to win. You *win* a poker game. You don't speak of *defeating* the other players. But even in chess, where you do speak of defeating your opponent, you don't claim that the object of the game is to *make* the other person lose. In MONOPOLY, however, that is precisely the object: to *make* everyone else lose.

On the face of it, this is rather hard to accept—or, at least, admit to. Certainly, the originators of MONOPOLY didn't admit to it. Just look at their statement of the object of the game. And maybe it's also true that very, very few of the 250 million people worldwide who own or have owned the game (and the millions more who play or have played it) face up to it, either. This would hardly be the first instance of mass delusion in history.

Elsewhere in this book we talk about negotiation, about making deals, about forging alliances, and even about playing cooperatively. We speak, too, about ethical play, about behaving well, and about the consequences of what might be called "corporate karma," the principle of what goes around comes around. All of this plays an important part in MONOPOLY, as it does in real life and in real business. But underneath it all, at the end of it all, is a zero-sum reality. Your winning requires others losing.

Elsewhere in this book we talk in depth about playing aggressively, even ruthlessly, and we present strategies and tactics, both practical and psychological, intended to accelerate the bankruptcy of everyone except you. But here and now is the place and time to decide whether you can deal with the core reality of MONOPOLY. For most of us, the game is sepia toned with the nostalgia of innocent childhood and tinged with a stroke of Americana. Nothing wrong there, as long as these emotions don't completely obscure the uncompromisingly competitive nature of the game. It is winner take all.

Community Chest

It's ridiculous to call this an industry—it's not. This is rat eat rat, dog eat dog.

—Ray Kroc, founder, McDonald's

Of course, this hard-edged attitude and take-no-prisoners approach need not be devoid of smiles or other indications that you and your competitors are actually enjoying yourselves. In fact, for many players of the game MONOPOLY as well as many players in the game of business, it is precisely this *hard edge* that creates a milieu in which a heightened sense of enterainment is possible. Still, others may find such intensity to be too much.

ABC

What does all this have to do with me? you might well ask. *I'm not about to be driven over the edge by a game of* MONOPOLY. *Let's just play!*

The point is this: If you start a MONOPOLY game "for fun," you are passing the time, sure enough, and maybe even quite pleasantly. But don't deceive yourself into thinking that you are playing the game.

In the 1992 movie version of David Mamet's brilliant play about selling and selling out, *Glengarry Glen Ross*, Alec Baldwin, as an abusively in-your-face motivational consultant, drills into the heads of a flagging sales crew a simple mantra: *A, B, C: Always Be Closing.*

Now, the Baldwin character is one extremely unpleasant man, a motivator from hell, whose only motivational tool is humiliation and whose only visual aid is a pair of brass balls he pulls out of his brief case and displays provocatively ("You know what it takes to sell real estate? It takes brass balls to sell real estate"). But cut through his harrowing sarcasm, and there is a lot of merit to the ABC formula.

It means that the successful salesperson always keeps before him the object of his game: closing the sale. Not one action is taken, not one word is uttered without that object in view. From first contact with a prospect, anything said or done that does not contribute to the close is wasted effort at best and, at worst, destructive of the sale.

Chance

For me, coming second is the same as coming last.

—Lew Grade,
British entrepreneur

The winning MONOPOLY player approaches the game from that same ABC perspective. Everything done is done with final object in view. This presupposes, of course, that the winning player understands the real object of the game—to force everyone else into bankruptcy—and accepts it.

Understanding and accepting this object, the winner always closes in on it. Each decision is shaped by this object. The question is not *Can I afford* TENNESSEE AVENUE? Nor is it even *Will buying* TENNESSEE AVENUE *help me win?* It is *How will buying* TENNESSEE AVENUE *help me bankrupt the other players? Should I buy it now? Or is there an alternative that will be even more effective in bankrupting everyone else?*

Chance

Always play to drive another player out of the game as quickly as possible.

—Dana Terman, 1977 and 1979 U.S. Monopoly Champion

Knowing the real object of MONOPOLY is the first step toward winning the game. Accepting that object, the consequences it entails, and the feelings it creates, is a second step. Developing the ability to maintain focus on the real object, to harness it as the source and guide of all your moves, is the third step to winning.

OF BUSINESS AND SCHNAPPS

There is an old German saying, "Business is business, and schnapps is schnapps." Is it one thing to be ruthlessly focused on the reality of the MONOPOLY game and altogether a different matter to "play" the same way in real-life business?

There is no one answer to this question, but it is no accident that people in business often play competitively together: golf, squash, tennis, poker, whatever. It is no accident that they often speak in metaphors drawn from sports, especially football. At some level, most of us recognize a connection between how one plays and how one works. A focused golfer, we observe, might have the kind of focus the firm needs in a consulting accountant. An aggressive tennis player might just have the right stuff to sell the new line before the competition gets to the same prospects. At some level, too, we see business as a game, with rules (official and unofficial), with strategies, with tactics, and, most of all, with winners and losers. Know the object of your game, accept that object, then know and accept what you must do to attain it.

Dumb luck is real. At least sometimes. Sometimes, players really do stumble to victory in MONOPOLY, just as some folks stumble to the top in business, like the sleepwalker in a silent cinema slapstick comedy who walks in traffic and on the parapets of tall buildings, oblivious, unconscious, and unharmed.

It's just that the odds are stacked so high the other way. In life, the unconscious almost always get flattened, the clueless business person tends to have a very brief career, and the MONOPOLY player who learns nothing about the game loses—again and again.

Community Chest It's part of the psychology of the game of preparation. You have to know each player and each team.

—Mark Cuban, owner, Dallas Mavericks

INFORMATION, PLEASE

In some endeavors, information is practically everything. In MONOPOLY, all the information in the world will not guarantee you victory. Chance and the skill of other players constitute a very heavy hand. Nevertheless, information gives you a tangible edge.

In MONOPOLY, as in any competitive enterprise, information is of at least five kinds:

1. *Environmental*: What are the rules of the game, written and otherwise? What are the odds of landing on any given property? In business, what are the market conditions? What is the business climate?

2. *Resources—yours*: What are your assets and liabilities? Strengths and weaknesses? Cash and property on hand?

3. *Resources—theirs*: What do you know about your competitors' assets and liabilities of all kinds? The etiquette of MONOPOLY prescribes that all players keep their assets—cash and title deeds—clearly visible. The reason? So that all can keep track of what everyone has.

4. *Goals and attitude—yours*: The Delphic Oracle put it in just two words: Know thyself. Know what you're about. What are your goals? How committed are you to achieving them? Do you feel like a winner? Are you a self-doubter? What are your spiritual and attitudinal strengths and weaknesses?

5. *Goals and attitude—theirs*: To the degree that you can, determine the objectives and goals of your opponent. Equally important, try to get inside your opponent's head and heart. What does he think? What does he feel?

ANTICIPATING YOUR OPPONENT

This last area of information is doubtless the most difficult to penetrate in any truly useful way. The greatest military commanders always made it their business to learn as much as they could about the character and habits of the opposing commander. If you've seen the great 1970 film biography *Patton*, starring George C. Scott as the most controversial American general of World War II, you may recall that General Patton, about to do battle with the legendary German tank commander Erwin Rommel, devoured Rommel's own writings on tactics, even as Rommel, in his headquarters, commissioned a subordinate officer to research the biography and character of Patton.

Chance The better people think they are, the better they will be. Positive self-image creates success.
—Liisa Joronen, CEO of SOL (Finland)

In business or any competitive enterprise, it is always useful to be able to *read* your opponents and competitors. Doing so will enable you to anticipate your opponent, and proactive, anticipatory steps are almost always more effective than steps taken in reaction to the move of another. Acting in anticipation confers far more leverage than acting in reaction. Hence the old saw about an ounce of prevention being worth a pound of cure.

READING YOUR OPPONENTS

Like any other game, MONOPOLY may be played with strangers, but unless you are engaged in an international MONOPOLY tournament (and there really is such a thing), you will probably play the game mostly with friends and family—people you know.

Use this knowledge. If you know that Joe is usually cautious, you may decide to err slightly on the side of caution, allowing yourself to keep more cash in reserve than you might otherwise do. On the other hand, if Jill has always seemed impulsive to you, maybe that's your cue to acquire property as fast and furiously as you possibly can, cash be damned, lest she shut you out.

But you don't need to be acquainted with your opponents to gain insight into them. A few trips around the board reveal much, provided that you are sensitive to the signals.

Does Joe hesitate when an opportunity presents itself? Does Jill buy absolutely everything, regardless of cost and cash on hand? Is Sam always counting his money? Do Pete's purchases make *any* sense at all?

TOKENS AS TOTEMS

Nor do you even have to wait until the first move is made before you begin to read your opponents. Consider: By what we *say*, we may either reveal *or* conceal ourselves. What we *choose*, however, is almost always a revelation. This is the principle behind the famous Rorschach "inkblot" test psychologists have long used. Test subjects are shown a series of symmetrical ink blots—abstractions that, in themselves, represent nothing—and are asked to say what they "see" in each image. They are asked, that is, to *choose* a meaning, and from that choice, the psychologist draws conclusions as to the subject's mental state, character, and attitude.

Chance

[Place] yourself in the shoes of your opponents to understand how they will counter your tactical moves.

—Raymond Smith, chairman, Rothschild North America, Inc.

The Rorschach equivalent in MONOPOLY are the tokens, the pieces the players move around the board.

Over the years, different editions of MONOPOLY have included various special tokens, and special MONOPOLY editions include special sets of tokens. But the standard game invariably includes at least ten:

- The flatiron
- The wheelbarrow
- The man astride a rearing horse
- The cannon
- The top hat
- The race car
- The battleship
- The Scottie

- The thimble
- The old shoe

Picking a token is the very first choice—the very first revelation—each player makes.

Does each token have a precise symbolic meaning? Of course not.

And it is also true that once a token is chosen, it is no longer available to other players. That is, if both Joe and Jill lust after the cannon, but Joe chooses it first, you will never know that Jill's first choice would have been the cannon as well. So it must be conceded that the tokens are inherently flawed as a Rorschach test (although it is possible that Jill will gasp, "Ugh! I wanted that piece," and thereby reveal herself).

Chance

I like to quickly get acquainted with my opponents and build relationships with them.

—Christopher Woo,
1995 MONOPOLY
World Champion

Yet despite their flaws as indicators of personality, attitude, and approach to the game, try thinking of the tokens as personal totems. So-called "primitive" peoples and members of various tribal societies have traditionally chosen or been assigned symbols, totems—often, totem animals—to express the content of their spirit. So and so is a wolf. Another person is designated a lion. Yet another, a serpent.

In our own "advanced" society, we adopt personal totems all the time: in the clothes we wear, in the accessories we wear (jewelry and the like), in the style of our hair, in the car we drive, and in the house we live in, not to mention the bumper stickers we may display on our cars or even the occasional tattoo we may acquire. One man spends $40,000 on a Corvette. Another spends that money on a minivan and a Taurus. Which one do you invite to your cocktail party? Which one do you ask for advice on life insurance?

THE TOKENS DECODED

Pay attention, then, when it comes time to pick the tokens. The choices are not accidental. Here are some ideas.

The flatiron, thimble, and wheelbarrow are domestic, non-aggressive choices, quiet choices. In a society painfully attuned to political correctness, it may be taking a risk to say that men rarely choose the thimble or flatiron. But, the fact is, they rarely do. The main point about these three tokens is that they are the "totems" of the conservative, perhaps even the timid.

The top hat and the Scottie are the most whimsical of the MONOPOLY tokens, and the player who chooses them proclaims a playful attitude toward the game, an attitude that is ultimately somewhat detached. There is nothing wrong with this. MONOPOLY, after all, is a game. But the most serious competitors rarely choose these two tokens.

The cannon, the man on the rearing horse, the battleship, and the race car are the most aggressive tokens in MONOPOLY. Players who choose these mean business—or, at least, they believe they do. Males often choose the cannon, the race car, or the battleship, while the man on the rearing horse is favored by girls and women. The woman who opts for the cannon, race car, or battleship can be counted on as a serious competitor—or, at the very least, someone intent on sending a deliberately com-

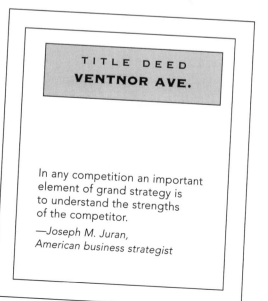

TITLE DEED
VENTNOR AVE.

In any competition an important element of grand strategy is to understand the strengths of the competitor.
—Joseph M. Juran,
American business strategist

petitive message, which, really, amounts to the same thing.

This leaves us with the old shoe. It is cute and old-fashioned, but also worn out. It is the antithesis of aggression. Were it a fancy boot, it could be interpreted as the totem of—what can we say—a kick-ass player. But it is, in fact, a worn-out old shoe, the kind a hobo would wear, and choosing this implies a feeling that you, like a hobo, are born to lose. This is the footwear—and the totem—of poverty and bankruptcy. It is not necessarily the token of a loser, but it does suggest that the person who chooses it believes he or she will not win.

CHOOSE YOUR TOKEN

All of the foregoing begs the question: *What token should I choose?*

The answer might depend on how you feel, and, in that case, your choice could tell you a thing or two about yourself. However, the more effective course is not to focus too much on how you feel, but instead, on what message you want to send the other players. You'll need to decide whether you want to present yourself as aggressive and serious, or as playful, or as passive, or perhaps as something of a sad sack, the wearer of the old shoe.

Which of these messages would be the most useful for you?

If you intend to play aggressively, consider sending out a deceptive message with the thimble or flatiron or even the old shoe. This may be just what you need to put your opponents off guard. On the other hand, if you feel the need to dominate and intimidate, the race car, cannon, battleship, or the man on the rearing horse will begin to telegraph that message.

AWARENESS IS ALL

In the end, the message we send may be less important than our purpose in sending it and our awareness that it is, in fact, being sent. Reject the notion that the choices you and others make are accidental. Regard them, instead, as messages, some transmitted consciously, some unawares, but all rich with information about emotion, character, attitude, direction, and degree of determination.

Chance

If you think you can, you can. And if you think you can't, you're right.

—Mary Kay Ash, founder, Mary Kay Cosmetics

All of these points clearly translate into the world of business, as well. You send messages every day and in every way, from the obvious to the subtle. You must be aware of the messages you're sending, and if you're really on top of things, you should be manipulating those messages for your benefit. Likewise, you need to maintain a level of alertness at all times in order to receive the messages that others in the business world are transmitting. Doing so gives you a clear and constant edge. Failing to do so is just another opportunity lost.

LESSON 18:

GAIN THE WORLD *AND* LOSE YOUR SOUL?

Assuming all players know the rules and are attentive throughout the game, it is not very easy to cheat at MONOPOLY, but it is possible. You might, for example, embezzle cash from the Bank when no one is looking. You could even steal from another player. Or you might deftly draw a known CHANCE or COMMUNITY CHEST card from the bottom of the deck.

Community Chest It is in our own interests that our social norms put common interests above the interests of the individual.

—George Soros, American financier

CHEATING WORKS

Cheating can certainly give you the edge in MONOPOLY, just as theft can give you the edge in life. If you steal money (and don't get caught), you have more money. If you can successfully manipulate or rig any business process (and you don't get caught), you almost certainly have a competitive advantage.

In MONOPOLY, you don't even have to cheat outright to gain an edge. You can simply be obnoxious.

For example, you might hide some of your title deeds or cash by letting them "slip" under the board, thereby misleading others or, at least, depriving them of information. You might attempt to intimidate others by your demeanor: offering insults ("Can't you *count?*"), expressing impatience ("Can we move sometime *before* sunrise?"), or being generally a bully ("If you were a real man, you'd sell me that property."). You might refuse to be helpful when someone asks a question about the rules ("I don't have time to teach you the rules"). You might rush the game in an effort to discourage an opponent from thinking through his move. Or this little piece of action: You throw doubles, land on an opponent's property, and immediately seize the dice for

Community Chest

Trust and similar values . . . have real, practical, economic value; they increase the efficiency of the system.
—Kenneth Joseph Arrow, American economist

your second throw—without giving the opponent an opportunity to open his mouth and demand the rent from you. Some players grab for the dice faster than shoppers go after the goods in a bargain-basement 10-minute sale.

All these actions, attitudes, and behaviors might well contribute to your winning a given game. But they are not ethical.

WHO NEEDS ETHICS?

So what?

Any game is a test of skill, an expedition into luck, and a measure of ethics. Most of us feel bad if we cheat or otherwise behave unethically. For many of us, avoiding that bad feeling is reason enough to act

Chance

A man I do not trust could not get money from me on all the bonds in Christendom.
—J. P. Morgan, American financier

ethically. Moreover, victory through cheating or distasteful behavior is a tainted victory. It never feels right, never feels whole or wholly earned.

CRIME AND PUNISHMENT

And, of course, there is always the risk of getting caught. In real life, getting caught may mean losing a client, losing a job, losing the respect of your colleagues, or maybe even going to jail. In MONOPOLY—well, do *you* want to be branded as someone who cheats at a board game?

Perform a "thought experiment," an exercise of the imagination:

Imagine yourself cheating. Imagine yourself caught. Imagine the first words out of your friends' mouths. More to the point: imagine the look on their faces.

Certain hard-nosed ultra-competitive business types will tell you that only weakness keeps you from cheating, and that embarrassment is not a good enough reason to refrain from something that could deliver the game to you. Well, do the thought experiment, and decide for yourself.

Community Chest

I never thought of losing, but now that it's happened, the only thing is to do it right.
—Muhammad Ali, American boxer

PRODUCTIVE ETHICS

Beyond feeling right and avoiding outright punishment or "mere" embarrassment, there is another good reason for behaving and playing ethically. Perhaps it is the most compelling reason of all.

Cheating and other unethical conduct are not sustainable. They cannot constitute a viable business policy.

You can win a game or two by cheating, but, unless you devote yourself to it, you cannot win consistently—even if you aren't caught. Get caught, of course, and it's game over. No one will want to play with you again. It won't be a question of winning or losing, but of not even being allowed into the game.

Much the same is true about obnoxious—albeit not even illegal—play. If you rush, if you browbeat, if you belittle, if you insult, you may be able to get through a game, but you probably won't be asked to play again, let alone again and again.

Ethical sales professionals are more successful than unethical sales professionals. While the cheat may make a sale, the ethical seller makes a customer. As soon as either professional makes a sale, it ends. But if it is a bad sale, it poisons the well and makes future sales difficult or impossible. In contrast, a customer treated ethically usually results in any number of future sales. Ethics is about creating relationships, and it is relationships that create business, now and over time. Good business generates more good business. Bad business is self-limiting, an end to business.

Community Chest

Making money doesn't oblige people to forfeit their honor or their conscience.
—Baron Rothschild, French philanthropist and tycoon

Good MONOPOLY generates more good MONOPOLY. If you play ethically—which means considerately, graciously, and honestly—you invite future games. This does not require you to play any less aggressively. By all means, play to win. But play in a manner that makes the experience of play enjoyable for all. *The Monopoly Companion* author Philip Orbanes puts it well: "Present yourself as the type of player others won't mind losing to."

An ethical game creates good feelings, win or lose. Lose to an ethical player, and you get up from the game board feeling you've fought the good fight. Lose to a jerk, and you feel robbed and cheated. Which you were.

In the previous lesson we learned this: Victory at any cost is no victory. Cheat or make yourself somehow obnoxious, and you impose limits on yourself that you may never be able to get beyond. Even if you win a game, you may find that you have forfeited the right ever to play again.

Community Chest

I've always realized that if I'm doing well at business I'm cutting some other bastard's throat.

—*Kerry Packer, Australian entrepreneur, chairman, Consolidated Press Holdings*

THE LIMITS OF ETHICS

Ethical play, in MONOPOLY as in business, does not mean diluting the will to win. It means defining victory ethically and, within that definition, devoting your efforts to winning, to playing fairly but ruthlessly.

The rules of MONOPOLY level the playing field. So far as material resources go, everyone is equal at the start of play. That is the only mercy prescribed by the rules of this game. If you would win, you must commit yourself to making the others lose. Victory in MONOPOLY does not mean that you come out *better* than the others, i.e. richer and with more property. It means that you have *eliminated* everyone else.

That is how winning is defined. To underscore this message of victory-by-elimination, the rules specifically bar players from helping one another: "No player may borrow from or lend money to another player." Moreover, while you are permitted—and encouraged—to trade property with another player, you cannot trade a favor or immunity for property: "Let me have PARK PLACE, and I won't charge you rent on my monopoly." This is against the rules, which allow no mercy except for initial equality.

ZERO-SUM? SOMETHING LIKE IT

Played properly—that is, in an ethical spirit—MONOPOLY is fun for everyone. The end, therefore, is not the sum total of the game. The play's the thing, as Shakespeare said, and even if you lose, you should have a good time doing so. In this sense, and this sense only, MONOPOLY need not be looked upon as zero-sum game. Everyone gains something. If this weren't true, the game would have been dead on arrival when it was introduced seventy some years ago. With all America in a depression, who needed more misery?

Chance

In business we cut each others' throats, but now and then we sit around the same table and behave. . . .
—Aristotle Onassis, Greek shipping tycoon

This said, the fact remains that MONOPOLY allows for only one winner. And that winner wins by making everyone else lose.

THE STING OF VICTORY

In an Olympic track event, a whole range of athletes may all perform at record-breaking levels and all emerge with glory. True, there is only one gold medal awarded, but that hardly means the others were defeated. In MONOPOLY, however, those others *are* defeated, and the winner is the last one standing.

It feels good to win. But how does it feel to make others lose?

MONOPOLY is a family favorite, regarded as wholesome and harmless. Nevertheless, it pivots upon ruthlessness. For what better measure of ruthlessness is there than the willingness to force others out of the game? MONOPOLY is not football or boxing. There's no physical contact here. You aren't expected to tackle or beat your opponent into submission. Yet it is nonetheless a game that tests each player's will to compete in a fight to the finish. Make no mistake: In a three-person game, the first person out can feel awfully lonely. For him, the party's over—and *you* put an end to it.

For the losers, MONOPOLY packs an unmistakable sting. You're *out* of the game, a game in which you may have already invested one, two, maybe three hours, a game that may go on for quite some time without you.

Avoiding this fate should be a keen spur to victory, to playing to win. Nevertheless, some find it painful to push others out of the fun. They'd almost rather lose themselves. They empathize with the other person. They think: *This just isn't worth it.*

If you would win at MONOPOLY, you need to resist the urge to be a nice guy, to hold back, to avoid or delay the elimination of your opponents. The sting of defeat, defeat as exclusion, is part and parcel of MONOPOLY. It must be accepted as a consequence of the game. In accepting it, the players are bound in a kind of covenant. They've agreed that there will be x losers and 1 winner.

MAKING THE COVENANT

All competitive endeavors partake of a similar covenant. Not all enterprises are strictly zero-sum, but almost all involve, to some degree, succeeding at the cost of another. Your attempt to alter this equation by letting up, dogging it, or even taking a dive will not succeed. You may lose, but the nature of the game will remain the same.

If, however, you choose to play—*and* choose to win—you must sign on to the covenant, compete, and do whatever damage is necessary.

Play ethically. Play ruthlessly. If this sounds contradictory, please review Lesson 18 and Lesson 19. Ethical behavior empowers the continuity of business. The ruthless will to win drives excellence in each encounter.

Now, add a third element: cooperation.

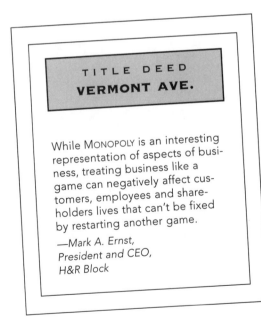

TITLE DEED
VERMONT AVE.

While MONOPOLY is an interesting representation of aspects of business, treating business like a game can negatively affect customers, employees and shareholders lives that can't be fixed by restarting another game.
—Mark A. Ernst,
President and CEO,
H&R Block

CAPITALIST CONTRADICTIONS

If it's hard enough to believe that you can be both ethical and 14ruthless, it seems downright impossible to accept the proposition that you can be both ruthless and cooperative. Nevertheless, this proposition has been the driving force behind commerce for a very long time. It's called capitalism.

Think about it. The capitalist system is based on—what should we call it? a mixture? a balance? a hodgepodge?—of cooperation and ruthless competition. Competitors cooperate in various initiatives that are "good for the industry" or that are perceived to be good for business, even as they strive to drive each other out of the market. If they get too cooperative, the government may step in with antitrust legislation. If they get too competitive, the government may step in with accusations of unfair competition or predatory practices. No wonder such eminently logical thinkers as Karl Marx and Vladimir Ilych Lenin sought to tear down the wildly contradictory capitalist system.

Community Chest

Be nice to people on your way up because you'll meet 'em on your way down.

—Wilson Mizner, American hotelier

Of course, thinkers like Marx and Lenin failed to understand that *complex* human activity is not *simply* logical. Take commerce, for example. It stubbornly refuses to be reduced to the simple Marxist formula, "From each according to his abilities, to each according to his needs." Human motivation is not driven by such simple logic, no matter how appealing. This being the case, how can one expect a system built of and by millions of human beings to be simply and straightforwardly logical?

The trouble with communism and other attempts to reduce commerce, the economy, or society itself to logical, non-contradictory order is that these systems of thought either attempt to kill or try to ignore the dynamic nature of human relationships. Such relationships are not binary transactions, as in a computer program, but multifarious and fluid—in other words, dynamic. Multiply such dynamic relationships by several million, and you have a system (if we can still call it that) ungovernable by a handful of static rules.

Do you need proof? Well, just ask yourself: Where is the Soviet Union today? And just consider how the USSR managed to last as long as it did. Its collective biography is a seventy-year chronology of oppression, coercion, execution, and dictatorship. Communism endures only by force—in effect, by cheating, by breaking all the rules of the game, so that there no longer is a game, but, rather, a collection of muffled lives lived out in a stagnant economy.

DEFINING COOPERATION

MONOPOLY models capitalism. Winning play calls for a combination of ruthless competition *and* willing cooperation.

Cooperation does not mean making formal or informal promises of immunity: "If you do such and such, I'll give you a free ride on my railroads." This is illegal. The antitrust division of the Department of Justice won't knock on your door to break up the game, but Parker Brothers just might. It's against the rules.

Cooperation does mean remaining open to trades with other players. *Lesson 13: Let's Talk*, discusses player-to-player trading. In general, you make a trade when you want a certain property. You make a trade when doing so seems especially advantageous to you. But consider broadening your definition of "advantageous" so that you make a lot of trades or, at least, as many trades as you possibly can. Whatever property you gain or give, whatever money you make or spend, there is a value to the act of trading in and of itself. In itself, the process of exchange creates a human relationship, a cooperative, collaborative bond.

WHY COOPERATE?

In MONOPOLY, you create cooperative relationships to gain property and—not to put too fine a point on it—to "gang up" on another player. Let's say there are three of you in the game. Bearing in mind that the object of the game is not so much to win, but to make others lose—that is, to squeeze others out of the game—it can be very useful to work with another player to keep a third player weak (that is, property poor) and force him or her out. Doing so gets you that much closer to attaining the object of the game.

In another instance, two players may "gang up" on the third if that third person is clearly making strides toward a position of extreme power that puts them on the fast track to victory.

TRULY LIMITED PARTNERSHIPS

Obviously, cooperative relationships are necessarily short lived in MONOPOLY. As soon as that third player is booted, you must now turn against your erstwhile "partner."

Moreover, you cannot be truly consistent in any alliance. Say you've been making a number of mutually advantageous trades with Joe. The two of you smile at each other when Jill lands on

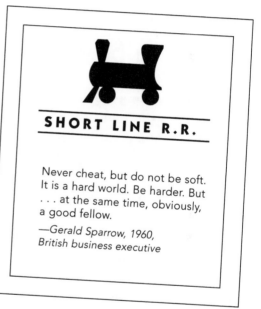

SHORT LINE R.R.

Never cheat, but do not be soft. It is a hard world. Be harder. But . . . at the same time, obviously, a good fellow.

—*Gerald Sparrow, 1960, British business executive*

your monopoly, which Joe's recent trade has enabled you to build. Now Jill is a big step closer to bankruptcy. But, in the next move, Joe lands on that very monopoly himself. Now he's not smiling. Even if you wanted to, you can't let Joe slide. The rules forbid it. He must pay. Right now, you look to Joe a lot less like an ally than an enemy, an opponent, just like Jill—only more menacing.

Will this drive Joe to target you by making trades with Jill?

It might. Especially if that would be a good thing for Joe. At the very least, it might afford him the momentary satisfaction of vengeance.

At best—from his perspective—making a trade with Jill might give Joe an opportunity to attack your position in the game, to drive you closer to bankruptcy. On the other hand, if trading with Jill merely strengthens her, keeps her in the game, both you *and* Joe are hurt.

In MONOPOLY, the tactics of cooperation are complex, delicate, and above all, subject to the dynamics of ever-changing player positions in the game. But while the tactics are always in flux, the principle of cooperation remains permanently viable, just as it does in the business world.

DOOM OF THE LONE WOLF

It is hard to go it alone in MONOPOLY, and it is just about impossible to do so in business. With customers and suppliers, you are well advised to form mutually beneficial, cooperative relationships.

Most of us do just that all of the time. However, avoid the error of confusing such relationships with friendship, love, or marriage. The terms of business relationships are subject to continual change, as the balance of supply and demand changes, as the condition and position of each party in the relationship changes, as needs change. When your supplier has a surplus of item x, you don't pay him a premium price for it just because you "have a relationship" with him. On the other hand, if you wish to preserve that relationship, it behooves you to resist the impulse to take him to the cleaners. You can offer a good deal for yourself that still represents something approaching a fair price for him.

COOPERATING WITH THE COMPETITION

More delicate are the relationships we forge with competitors. At times, it is useful to help one another out. Acme Company is short of shipping crates. They ask if they can purchase some of yours.

Do you refuse? Do you offer them in exchange for nothing less than an arm and a leg? Or do you work out a good deal for both of you?

It depends on what you need at the moment, and on how you want to structure the climate in which you do business on an ongoing basis. If there is business enough for everyone, you may want to make a deal. If, however, the climate is truly cutthroat, you may decide to sacrifice cooperation in the name of taking a harder line.

THE KARMA CONCEPT

Cooperation in MONOPOLY and in the world beyond the game board is not a matter of being a nice guy. Instead, it is a matter of advantage and benefit. Advantage and benefit need not be zero-sum commodities. Sometimes you share advantage and benefit with others, so cooperation is clearly called for. But even when your advantage and benefit are not immediately evident, don't be too hasty in turning down a call for cooperation.

Each positive business relationship you create, for however long you create it, generates what we may call corporate karma. In Buddhist thought, karma is a kind of universal spirit that informs all things and all acts. Each act of goodness and each act of wickedness works changes in karma. Translated into common-sense terms, the deal is this: *What goes around comes around.*

Chance

It's usually arrogance that brings you down.
—Michael Eisner, CEO, Disney Company

WEATHER REPORT

The environment in which we do business is characterized by a kind of karma. Some climates tend to be cooperative, others cutthroat, and most fall somewhere in between. I've used the word *climates* deliberately here. Climate is the prevailing range of weather in a particular place over time. Climate is relatively stable and predictable; however, within any given range of climate, the *weather* can vary dramatically from day to day and even hour to hour. You may be well aware of the climate that prevails in your business, but you'd also better be ready for sudden changes in the weather. Just because you try to create the good corporate karma of cooperation most of the time, you need not tie your hands in a particular situation that calls for strongly competitive behavior. Conversely, just because you often compete ruthlessly, you do not have to withhold cooperation for the sake of pure consistency.

JUST PLAIN MEAN

Bad corporate karma is not a product of capitalist competition. Consider this scenario: There are five suppliers of "widgets" in a given area. The covenant that operates among all five is based on the principle of business competition. That is, each business understands and accepts that it is in competition with the others. However, this understanding does not require a gratuitous refusal to cooperate when cooperation is beneficial to all. Such an attitude of non-cooperation, without regard to the "weather" of the moment, generates bad corporate karma. It is just plain mean, and it makes doing business that much more difficult for everyone. It's bad enough, of course, if all five suppliers act this way. But if you're the only S.O.B. in the bunch, you will, sooner or later, find yourself frozen out on the losing end of a four-to-one contest.

ACT IN MULTIPLE DIMENSIONS

The extent to which MONOPOLY mirrors and models the multidimensionality of business life is very striking indeed. Consider these last three lessons (18 through 20). Apply to MONOPOLY any *one* of them, to the exclusion of the others, and you invariably reduce your chances of playing a consistently winning game. Apply them *all*—ethics, ruthlessness, and cooperation—in a dynamic, responsive fashion, and you just as invariably increase your prospects for victory.

Baseball, the great American pastime, has given us some of the great American quotations. Casey Stengel believed the game pared priorities down to the essentials: "There are three things you can do in a baseball game. You can win, or you can lose, or it can rain." Babe Ruth brought to it his philosophy of life: "I hit big or I miss big, I like to live as big as I can." Hank Aaron used it to define a kind of dogged heroism: "My motto was always to keep swinging. Whether I was in a slump or feeling badly or having trouble off the field, the only thing to do was keep swinging." And Yogi Berra seemed to step through the diamond into a quirky dimension just a little different from our own: "Baseball is ninety percent mental. The other half is physical."

Even non-players said some pretty great things about the game. "Poets are like baseball pitchers," Robert Frost once observed. "Both have their moments. The intervals are the tough things." And the educator and cultural critic Jacques Barzun proclaimed: "Whoever wants to know the heart and mind of America had better learn baseball."

Chance

In business as on the battlefield, the object of strategy is to bring about the condition most favorable to one's own side.

—Kenichi Ohmae, Japanese management theorist

PROFUNDITY VIA BROOKLYN

But quite possibly the most profound words ever to come out of baseball were spoken by Branch Rickey, the legendary owner of the Brooklyn Dodgers, who, among other things, made moral history when he single-handedly desegregated major league baseball by hiring the great Jackie Robinson in 1947. "Luck," Rickey said, "is the residue of design."

Community Chest

It is a great skill to know how to guide your luck even while waiting for it.
—Baltasar Gracián, 17th century Spanish writer

It is a brilliant statement, but not a particularly easy one. Start taking it apart and see.

Does it mean that "luck" is actually the result of planning and strategy? Or does it mean that luck is what's left over after planning—that luck is the nasty "residue" planning can't quite dissolve?

Perhaps the quotation implies both meanings. We make our own luck, up to a point, but nothing we do can completely remove luck from the picture.

WHAT TO DO WITH THE RESIDUE

It is with this double sense in mind that we've now cruised through a score of lessons in MONOPOLY as a model for doing effective business. There are givens in the game—resources, equipment, rules, and, yes, luck, chance, call it what you will. No amount of strategic planning can circumvent these givens or completely control their effects. This does not mean, however, that planning is fruitless. Quite the contrary. A good plan will shape your luck to whatever extent it *can* be shaped in any given situation.

A GOOD PLAN

What goes into a good plan?

Let's begin with Branch Rickey's word, *design*. A good plan must be a good design. Now, a good design is functional; it gets the job done. This implies two essential first steps in starting to build a good design. First, know what you want to accomplish. Second, know what your resources are.

The order in which these two basics have been listed is not immutable and absolute. You may find yourself with an idea, a goal, and, from this, set off to gather the resources necessary to achieve it. Or you may find yourself with a set of resources, and your next job is to find a goal suitable to what you already have. A third course and a fourth synthesize these two alternatives: You have a certain goal, and you have certain resources, to which you must selectively add in order to achieve your goal. Or you have certain resources, and you have a certain goal, to which you must add or from which you must subtract to bring it into line with those resources.

Once you have aligned goal with resources or resources with goal, you have the foundation on which you can raise the superstructure of your design. That design must both withstand and make productive use of whatever it encounters, whatever is thrown at it. You cannot know in advance everything that will happen, but you can learn enough to make intelligent predictions to sketch out the parameters within which the design is intended to survive and to function.

Chance Facts are the most important thing in business. Study facts and do more than is expected of you.
—Frederick Hudson Ecker, chairman, Metropolitan Life Insurance

THE SAGA OF GALLOPING GERTIE

On July 1, 1940, following two years of construction, the 5,939-foot-long Tacoma Narrows Suspension Bridge, linking Tacoma, Washington, with Gig Harbor over Puget Sound, was opened to traffic. Almost immediately, motorists dubbed it "Galloping Gertie," because it rolled and undulated in the wind. As they traversed its 2,800-foot center span, drivers often reported feeling as if they were on an ocean voyage. They watched the cars ahead disappear momentarily then reappear, descending into the trough of a great sea swell, then rising up again.

Community Chest

Few people realize that luck is created. Just as money is.

—Robert T. Kiyosaki, author of *Rich Dad, Poor Dad*

On November 7, 1940, during a windstorm, Galloping Gertie began to undulate wildly. An intrepid newsreel cameraman recorded its tortured twisting, the ribbon of highway behaving like some giant Mobius strip. At about 11 a.m., as winds hit 42 miles per hour, the bridge violently corkscrewed itself apart. The collapse was total.

A QUESTION OF DESIGN

A 42-mile-per-hour wind is a very stiff gale, but it is hardly a freak of nature or a stroke of bad luck. It is one of the givens in a particular environment. It is written into the rules of a particular game. Whatever enters into that environment, whatever engages those rules, must be designed to survive usefully within that environment and according to those rules. The Tacoma Narrows Suspension Bridge did not meet these standards. Without sufficient regard for the aerodynamics of the environment, engineers built a conventional suspended plate-girder bridge, a design that caught the wind instead of letting the wind pass through it. When the wind became sufficiently intense, the bridge undulated in the current. Fatally.

A design that respected and addressed the aerodynamics of the Narrows would not have altered nature. The windstorm of November 7, 1940, would still have occurred, as would others, later, with even higher winds. But such a design would have permitted the bridge to survive.

LESSON LEARNED

The hard lesson of Galloping Gertie was not lost. A new, thoroughly redesigned Tacoma Narrows Bridge was opened on October 14, 1950, and has been carrying traffic ever since. No one said, *We're just too unlucky. Forget about a bridge.* No one said, *The Narrows are just too unpredictable. Forget about a bridge.* Instead, the engineers studied, learned, accepted all the givens, and came up with a plan better suited to them.

THE VALUE OF IMPERFECT KNOWLEDGE

In *Lesson 3: A Roll of the Dice,* we tackled the issue of chance, demonstrating that the result of tossing two six-sided dice was not truly random, but, in fact, predictable, albeit within limits. If your goal is to win a MONOPOLY game, it is helpful to know your odds of rolling a particular number in a particular circumstance. Is this knowledge infallible? No. Does it ensure victory? Of course not. Does it alter the odds? Hardly.

But it does allow for the creation of a design better suited to at least one of the givens of the game: moves dictated by the roll of dice.

Similarly, in *Lesson 9: A Random Walk*, we began a discussion of what you can expect on each trip around the MONOPOLY board. In the next two lessons (22 and 23), we'll elaborate on that earlier discussion. Right now, the point is this: A limited number of things can happen each time around the board. It is possible to become thoroughly familiar with those things and what they mean to the outcome of the game. It is also possible to predict—albeit to a very limited degree—which of those things is most likely to happen at any given time.

You can learn quite a bit about the range of possibilities and probabilities in MONOPOLY. Nevertheless, the best knowledge that you can acquire is limited and, at that, also of limited practical value. Still, imperfect and incomplete knowledge is always preferable to perfect and total ignorance.

We each of us launch enterprises into regions more or less beyond our control. What knowledge we are able to acquire enables the creation of a plan, which, in turn, creates some luck while also leaving a stubborn and irreducible residue of luck we didn't create. Don't mistake that knowledge for victory. All knowledge can do is guarantee a fight. Ignorance, on the other hand, offers nothing better than surrender.

Community Chest

We must believe in luck. For how else can we explain the success of those we don't like?
—Attributed to Jean Cocteau, French writer

Horatio Alger, who lived from 1832 to 1899, was the author of some 100 books that sold, during his lifetime, in excess of 20 million copies. Clearly, his work stuck a proverbial nerve, and it was so popular and pervasive that his name entered the English language. We now call the rags-to-riches biography of any self-made person a "Horatio Alger story."

The Horatio Alger story, we have been taught to believe, is a quintessentially *American* story because "America is the land of opportunity," a place unique in the world, where a person can be anything he or she wants. All that's required is hard work.

THE HORATIO ALGER LIE

And this is where the Horatio Alger story becomes—well, we could use a culturally highfalutin term and say that this is where the Horatio Alger story becomes an "American myth." Or we could just put it in a more down-to-earth manner: *This is where the Horatio Alger story becomes a lie.*

It's a lie most of us buy into, some of us for a very long time, others lifelong. The lie is this: *Hard work will reward you with wealth.*

The lie is twofold.

First, the truth is that, by itself, hard work is not sufficient to achieve success in any enterprise. Work hard and stupid, for instance, and you will probably come out with very little for your pains. The formula *Hard work will reward you with wealth* is a case of magical thinking. It turns on that word "reward," as if hard work were some ironclad contract entitling one to wealth. Look around. Some of the poorest people you know work the hardest.

That brings us to the second part of the lie. It is easy to find opportunities for hard work. Any number of employers are willing to give you all the hard work you want. But the hard fact is that very, very few people become wealthy by working—hard or not—for an employer.

Our teachers and our parents tell us to study hard, get a good education, then go out and find a good job and a good company to work for. It's very bad advice, though well meaning. The truth is that a life of hard work is simply too easy to be an effective formula for accumulating significant wealth. The most you can reasonably hope for from a job—that is, wage work done for an employer—is survival. You may make a fair amount of money, but you will rarely become wealthy.

Chance

Devote the same earnest attention to investing that $50,000 as you devoted to earning it.

—Ivan Boesky, American financier

THE WAY OF WEALTH

Let's look at wealth. Being rich is not the same as being wealthy. Wealth is money you do not need to live on, so that it becomes available for investment. That is, wealth is money that produces more money. Not all rich people are wealthy. Many spend their money and buy quite wonderful things, so that there are plenty of rich people who scarcely make ends meet. A wealthy person, in contrast, invests most of his or her money, so that it will create more money. He or she may set aside some cash to buy wonderful things—provided that doing so does not eat into the wealth, the money that generates more money.

Working for a wage takes time, time that could otherwise be invested in creating wealth. The harder you work for a wage, the more wealth-building time you lose.

INVESTMENT VERSUS SPENDING

But how do you work at creating wealth?

There are many ways. You might create and manage your own business. Or you might devote time and energy to discovering and researching promising investments. Or you might just make it your full-time business to find those investments. However you go about it, the objective is the same: You need to identify, develop, and manage various means by which you can invest rather than spend money.

For example: You find that you have five thousand "extra" dollars. You can buy a high-end, big-screen television, you can pony up a down payment on a luxury car, you can put the money in the bank, or you can search for an investment. The first two options provide pleasure, but at a cost. Buying the television spends the money, which makes it unavailable for the purposes of wealth. Using the money as a down payment on an expensive car costs even more. Not only have you made the money unavailable as wealth, you've figured out a way to use it to acquire a liability. True, on a balance sheet, a nice automobile would be penciled into the asset column. But, in truth, it costs you, and costs you some more. That $5,000 is only the first payment of many.

Community Chest

It takes a passionate commitment to really thoroughly understand something. . . . Most people don't take the time to do that.

—Steve Jobs, CEO, Apple, Inc.

Then there is the third option. Putting the money in the bank is safe because, among other things, banks are federally insured. But putting your $5,000 in the bank is no investment. Bank interest rates are usually much lower than the potential return on riskier investments. In truth, by putting the money in the bank, you are doing little more than parking it. If you know you're going to need that $5,000 to live on, this is not a bad idea. But, remember, in this hypothetical case, we are assuming the $5,000 is "extra" money. You *don't* need it to live on.

So we come to the investment option. By putting the $5,000 at risk, you use it as wealth and you attempt to grow it. Of course, you may also lose it, but if you invest the time (and not just the money) in acquiring information, identifying promising opportunities, then choosing and managing the opportunity you select, you will minimize your risk.

Wealth is acquired not through working for another, but by working for yourself. This may mean starting your own business, or it may mean investing time in identifying good investments and then using money not to buy liabilities, but to acquire assets—things that will add to your income rather than deplete it.

INVESTMENT, MONOPOLY® STYLE

Okay. Fine. Not just investment, but well-researched investment— the product of an investment of time as well as money—is the way to wealth. What does this have to do with MONOPOLY? After all, in MONOPOLY, you can only invest in what you land on or what goes up for auction. The range of your investments is limited to the handful of properties on the board. Besides, as a general rule, it's best just to buy up whatever you can whenever you can. As far as the properties paying off, it's the luck of the roll. If others land on your monopolies, you make money. If not, you don't.

So the question is this: MONOPOLY models a lot of business skills and situations, but does it fall short where investment is concerned? Does the model break down?

For the casual player, it does indeed fall short. How can you research MONOPOLY properties, which, when all is said and done, are nothing more than words and symbols on a board? There is no real pavement on MONOPOLY streets. There are no real houses, no living, breathing residents, no realtors, no city, even.

In contrast to the casual player, the serious player understands that the absence of all these things does not eliminate the need for research, but it does reduce it to a few essentials, which nevertheless yield an estimate of the return on investment (ROI) for each property.

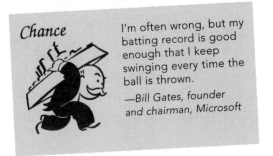

Chance

I'm often wrong, but my batting record is good enough that I keep swinging every time the ball is thrown.

—Bill Gates, founder and chairman, Microsoft

To calculate the ROI for a given monopoly, you need to know the following:

- Cost to acquire the monopoly
- Cost to build on the monopoly
- Payoff on the built-up monopoly
- Likely frequency with which an opponent will land on the monopoly

The first two items are easy enough to calculate, but, in themselves, they hardly constitute enough information on which to base a wise investment decision. They tell you about price, not about value. They tell you what your investment will cost, not what wealth that investment may produce.

The last two items, taken with the first two, yield an assessment of the value of the investment. Unfortunately, they are much more difficult to calculate. Fortunately, somebody else has already done all the work and published the results. The centerpiece of *The Monopoly Companion*, the book MR. MONOPOLY "told to" Philip Orbanes, consists of "tip sheets," which assess the value of each monopoly in terms of cost to build, frequency of hits, and payoff—the latter expressed in the percent of investment the owner of a given monopoly regains each time an opponent completes a trip around the board. (The payoff percentage calculation is based on there being three houses on each property in the monopoly.)

Let's cut to the chase. According to Orbanes's figures, the smartest properties (by color) to own are these:

- The oranges, with a frequency of 52.4 percent and a payoff of 25 percent
- The reds, with a frequency of 52 percent and a payoff of 19 percent
- The yellows, with a frequency of 47 percent and a payoff of 18 percent
- The light purples, with a frequency of 46 percent and a payoff of 19 percent

We'll get into the "non-color" properties—railroads and utilities—in Lesson 24. Here and now, however, the point of this lesson is to visualize MONOPOLY as a three-dimensional model of investment for the purpose of building wealth.

Dimension one is the range of available opportunities and their cost. There are 22 streets in MONOPOLY, no more, no fewer.

Dimension two is your available money resources.

Dimension three is the time and effort you invest in assessing dimension one, and how dimension one and dimension two align (or fail to align) with one another. If you decide that your resources are inadequate to the investment opportunity that presents itself, you can shrug your shoulders and proclaim "I can't afford that." Or, you can extend the activities of dimension three to include researching how to change the phrase *I can't afford that* into an answer to this question: *What must I do to afford that?*

Community Chest

You can't measure the value of being first.

—*Chris Moore, British marketing director, Domino's*

INVESTING IN THE THIRD DIMENSION

Think about what dimension three implies in the world beyond the game board. In that world, there is a very broad but nevertheless limited range of opportunities (dimension one). You have limited financial resources (dimension two). And you have a limited fund of time to devote to researching dimension one and how it fits together with dimension two. The more time you can invest in research and management of your wealth, the more wealth you are likely to acquire. Therefore, dimension three, time, may be your most potent and, therefore, most valuable resource. Will you, then, squander it as Horatio Alger counsels, in "hard work" for some employer? Or will you husband it jealously and give it not to some employer, but to yourself, to invest in building *your* wealth on *your* terms?

We've said it over and over again. MONOPOLY is about opportunity. That means, unless you have a very compelling reason not to (in other words, your treasury is drained, your cupboard bare), you should buy whatever you can whenever you can. This being the case, a lesson on the "dumbest properties to own" promises the virtue of brevity.

IMMEDIATE VALUE AND POTENTIAL VALUE

Chance

It's important in the new economy to pay attention to increasing returns; so too in Monopoly.

—Professors Paul Farris and Phil Pfeifer, University of Virginia

All MONOPOLY properties have some immediate value and, often, significantly greater potential value. The potential value of MARVIN GARDENS is obvious if neither VENTNOR nor ATLANTIC AVENUES is owned. If you already own VENTNOR AVENUE, and ATLANTIC AVENUE is still free, the potential value of MARVIN GARDENS is, of course, even greater. The same is true if Joe owns VENTNOR and ATLANTIC AVENUES, and you land on MARVIN GARDENS. Depending on the players' relative positions in the game, it may be as important to block Joe's impending monopoly as it is to build one of your own.

The potential value of MARVIN GARDENS is much less obvious if one yellow is already owned and another still available, or if the other two yellows are held by two different players. Nevertheless, in both cases, MARVIN GARDENS still has potential. In the first instance, you may be able to trade with the other player for his yellow, then hope either to land on the other yellow or acquire it at auction. In a case where you hold one property of a color group, another player holds one, and one is still unowned, it is always best to trade with the other player *before* acquiring the unowned property. A player will be very reluctant to sell you the property she knows you need to complete a monopoly.

Community Chest The flaws of capitalism are people who don't know how to run businesses well. They waste capital. They wither it away.

—Steve Forbes, American publishing executive

Even if two yellows are already held by two players, you may be able to make a trade. The problem here is that, once you hold two of the three properties in a color group, as we've just observed, most players will be reluctant to sell you the third property you need to complete a monopoly. They may do so if they are in desperate straits. They may also do so for an exorbitant amount of money or a very juicy property swap. This is one reason why, as discussed in *Lesson 13: Let's Talk*, it's a good idea to trade frequently throughout the game. Looking to the future, bearing in mind the idea of ultimately putting together a monopoly, make trades to acquire at a bargain price properties without obvious potential value.

NO SUCH THING AS A DUMB PROPERTY?

So the point is this: It's pretty hard to buy a dumb property in MONOPOLY. Most are good to own.

It *is* possible to make dumb deals—to pay too much in a trade or to purchase properties of low potential value when you are hurting for cash.

Beyond this, you should be wary of the low-rent properties that seem like real bargains. The BALTIC AVENUE and MEDITERRANEAN AVENUE monopoly looks like a steal at $60 and $60, but, according to Orbanes's calculations, the dark purples have the lowest frequency of hits and, among the street properties, the lowest payoff percentage (see the previous lesson for an explanation of these concepts).

Each trip around the board, a player has a 24.8 percent chance of landing on a dark purple—as opposed to a 52.4 percent chance of hitting an orange. The payoff percentage for the dark purples is a paltry 14 percent. This means that, with three houses each on MEDITERRANEAN AVENUE and BALTIC AVENUE, you are likely to recover only 14 percent of your investment each time a player rounds the board. It is true that, at $620 maximum, the dark purples have the lowest possible investment cost of all the street properties, but if you rely on these properties to win, you'll be disappointed.

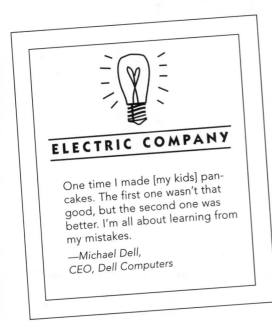

ELECTRIC COMPANY

One time I made [my kids] pancakes. The first one wasn't that good, but the second one was better. I'm all about learning from my mistakes.

—Michael Dell,
CEO, Dell Computers

On the other hand, throwing money at a set of properties and calling it an investment is not the wisest alternative. On the MONOPOLY spectrum, we think of the dark purples and the dark blues—BOARDWALK and PARK PLACE—as dwelling on the opposite ends of the economic spectrum. Actually, the true economic antithesis of MEDITERRANEAN and BALTIC AVENUES is not the dark blue group, but the greens: PENNSYLVANIA, NORTH CAROLINA, and PACIFIC AVENUES. Whereas the dark purples call for the least maximum investment at $620, it takes $3,920 to purchase the greens and put hotels on them, making this group the most expensive in MONOPOLY.

What do you get for your investment on the greens? You earn a modest 16 percent payoff. Six street properties—the oranges, the light blues, the reds, the light purples, the dark blues, and the yellows—offer greater payoffs. Only MEDITERRANEAN and BALTIC AVENUES have a lower payoff percentage, at 14 percent. (But, then, what do you expect for your $620?) A player has a 46.4 percent chance of landing on one of the greens each trip around the board. Of all the street properties, the prospects for a hit are greater with the oranges, reds, and yellows than with greens.

THE BEST IS THE ENEMY OF THE GOOD

Chance

I don't like the idea of getting comfortable.

—*Richard Branson, founder, Virgin Records and Virgin Airlines*

Does all this mean that the greens are dumb properties?

Well, they aren't the smartest investment, but, when they are landed on, they do pay handsomely. Still, it behooves a player to give top priority to the smartest properties, discussed in the previous lesson. Yet, as General George S. Patton famously observed, "The best is the enemy of the good." If you pass up the greens in the hope of acquiring, say, the oranges, you are spurning the good in quest of the best. This is not an effective strategy, because the good is always better than the bad, which, in MONOPOLY, is to be caught without any productive properties.

As in life, MONOPOLY rarely places in your lap the ideal opportunity. It does, however, offer myriad less-than-ideal, yet good, opportunities. Gather them up. For all their shortcomings, they are infinitely better than the absence of opportunity. The absolute, bottom-line dumbest property to own is no property at all.

The name of the game is MONOPOLY, and what that name brings to mind is ownership of all properties of the same color, street properties, ripe for building and sucking the cash out of your opponents—not in polite little sips, but in great, greedy gulps. No doubt about it, the glamour properties in MONOPOLY are the streets.

COLORLESS PROPERTIES

Which leaves the railroads and utilities—where?

Well, for many players, it leaves them in the dust. They are perceived as second-class properties, afterthoughts, really. You land on them, you buy them, but you're not really thrilled about them. They are, quite literally, colorless: a collection of plain black-and-white title deeds.

Is this a fair perception?

Maybe. Let's face it, the ELECTRIC COMPANY and the WATER WORKS are pretty lackluster. If one is owned, the player who lands on it must pay you four times the amount shown on the dice. That

Community Chest

Buy stocks like you buy your groceries, not like you buy your perfume.

—Warren Buffet,
American entrepreneur
and financier

means that if he threw a big twelve, you get $48. Not very exciting. Snake eyes will net you, oh, eight bucks. Own both the WATER WORKS and the ELECTRIC COMPANY, and a player who hits must pay ten times the number shown on the dice, so you could make as much as $120 (or as little as $20), which is still far from the two grand BOARDWALK with a hotel commands.

And it gets worse. *The Monopoly Companion* calculates that a player has a 32 percent chance of landing on a utility each time around the board. That puts it in eighth place for frequency among the properties. Only the dark blues (28.3 percent) and dark purples (24.8 percent) have lower hit rates. Payoff is at the *very* bottom of the heap: You can expect to regain a meager 7.5 percent of your investment each time an opponent completes a circuit of the board. And that is only if you own both utilities.

WELL, THE PRICE IS RIGHT . . .

No glamour and a low return. Why bother with the utilities?

In a contraction and a word, *They're cheap.* Each costs $150. In fact, the cost to own the utilities is the lowest of all developed properties in the game. That's because they're sold pre-developed. There are no houses or hotels to buy. Another plus is that you won't ever have to pony up a per-building tax or street-repair assessment on them.

They are *utilities.* That means they're useful, but unglamorous. They will produce modest returns steadily.

Likewise, there are plenty of investments in the real world of business that require little time or effort once they

Community Chest To last, a company must strive to add long-term value rather than going for the quick buck. . . .
—Charles G. Koch, chairman and CEO, Koch Industries

are in place, and that offer modest yet steady gains. As long as the time commitment does not outweigh the overall value, such investments can prove quite beneficial.

Community Chest

Nothing that costs only a dollar is worth having.
—Elizabeth Arden, American cosmetics manufacturer

RIDING THE RAILS

It is unfortunate that many players lump the railroads with the utilities. If the disdain with which the utilities are regarded is undeserved, it still must be conceded that they will never merit much enthusiasm. But the railroads should.

There are four railroads distributed around the board. In addition, two CHANCE cards direct players to "the nearest Railroad" and further direct them to pay the owner twice the rental to which he or she is entitled. There's also a "Take a Ride on the Reading" CHANCE card, which slightly increases the chances of hitting that property.

Now, turn again to Orbanes's calculations: Each trip around the board, a player has a whopping 64 percent chance of landing on a railroad, making these the highest-frequency properties in MONOPOLY. True, the payoff percentage is not staggering—16 percent, if all four railroads are owned—but it is only a little below the game average payoff percentage of 16.6 percent. As with utilities, the cost of ownership is low. Eight hundred dollars will buy you all four railroads. Only the dark purples and the utilities are cheaper.

The railroads are the cash cows of MONOPOLY. The payoff on any given hit may not be spectacular, but, as the old-time deejays put it, the hits just keep coming. If you can acquire two, three, or all four railroads, you will be in an excellent position to collect a steady stream of cash from each player.

CARPE DIEM, ANYONE?

Some years ago, the maker of a haircoloring product deluged the television airwaves with ads depicting gorgeous women tossing in silky slow motion their thick manes of vivid blonde hair. The kicker was the slogan: "If I have only one life, let me live it as a blonde." And the subtext was this: *Life is short. Grab the glamour.* The English poets of the late renaissance had another phrase for this philosophy. *Carpe diem,* they counseled. *Seize the day.* "Gather ye rosebuds while ye may."

It is a compelling philosophy, which sells a lot of luxury—extravagant clothing, expensive cars, "once-in-a-lifetime" vacations—and does not restrict sales to those who can readily afford such items. Plenty of people are in hock to their suburban villa or in servile bondage to their BMW. Who, after all, wants to be doomed to a drab, make-do life in sensible shoes? Better to live it as a blonde, regardless of the costs.

Chance

You don't go broke making a profit.

—Sir Nicholas Shehadie, Australian business executive

Yet if glamour bankrupts you, you're out of the game.

HORNS OF A DILEMMA

When life offers to put you on the horns of a dilemma, your best move is to politely decline to take a seat. You do not *have* to choose between the sensibly unexciting and the extravagantly glamorous. You *can* partake in some of both.

In targeting the big score, don't neglect the steady sources of cash. These leaven your investments. If you want the vehicle that is your life to be powered by 400 horses and eight cylinders wrapped in flashy sheet-metal, that's fine. Just don't neglect the springs, shocks, and tires, which will carry you along and smooth the journey.

In the previous lesson, we explored the folly of turning up your nose at the "colorless" properties, the resolutely mundane utilities and railroads. There is a pleasure in acquisition—even if it's only a title deed in a game of

Community Chest

I do not love the money. What I do love is the getting of it.
—Philip D. Armour, American business executive

MONOPOLY—and that pleasure is pegged to a sliding scale of perceived prestige. The WATER WORKS will never be the object of desire that is a BOARDWALK or a PARK PLACE.

THE PRESSURE OF EMOTION

Luxury goods, the high end, the blue chips, a prestigious address, an impressive automobile, all of these things excite desire, and desire drives ambition, drives achievement, and also drives decision. It's not all bad, of course, but it can blind us to the utilities and railroads, the fundamentals and basics that leaven any enterprise.

Possession creates emotional attachments that sometimes cause us to cling to things and to ideas long after they have ceased to be assets and have started to become liabilities. Anyone serious about trading stocks, for example, soon learns never to become emotional about those securities or the companies that underlie them. When it's time to sell, it is time to sell. Nor will it bring any benefit to get angry with a poor-performing stock. Your anger may prompt you to sell at precisely the wrong time.

What is true of stocks is true of most possessions, including the various ideas and enterprises in which we claim an ownership stake. When a business endeavor goes bad, it's often hard to let go, however necessary it may be to do so. When a favorite idea fails beyond fixing, it is time to shed it and move on.

THE MONOPOLY® MONITOR

If you don't think you're ever moved by emotion in making decisions that should be strictly business, try monitoring your MONOPOLY style.

What monopoly do you most desire? Which one do you consider virtually the same as victory?

BOARDWALK and PARK PLACE, of course. Everybody wants them. And, no doubt, the dark blues are valuable real estate to own. That's certainly not a figment of your imagination. But it is also true that owning this monopoly does not necessarily bring victory. In fact, most players who win, win without BOARDWALK and PARK PLACE. That's because they aren't particularly easy to acquire. To begin with, they're not very easy to land on. After all, there's only two of them, instead of the three street properties that make up all the other monopolies except for MEDITERRANEAN and BALTIC AVENUES. A player has a 28.3 percent chance of hitting BOARDWALK or PARK PLACE each trip around the board. That is the second lowest frequency percentage in the game,

Chance

Greed is even more contagious than fear.

—Bud Hadfield, founder, Kwik Kopy

Chance

It's a bit like being a race-horse—you like to win.

—Charles Brady, American investor

just above the dark purples. Moreover, BOARDWALK and PARK PLACE are traded reluctantly, and if they happen to come up for auction, bidding is generally fierce.

But let's say you do acquire the dark blue monopoly. You will want to build quickly and extravagantly. This is an expensive proposition, with houses priced at $200 each. You will also be tempted to focus your development exclusively on this monopoly rather than on something with greater potential productivity. Remember, there's only a 28.3 percent frequency of dark blue hits each time around the board. The payoff percentage for the BOARDWALK and PARK PLACE monopoly is 18 percent, lower than for the oranges (25 percent), the lowly light blues (22.4 percent), the reds (19 percent), and the light purples (19 percent).

No one is saying that BOARDWALK and PARK PLACE are bad investments. It's just that their prestige overshadows their real numbers. They aren't bad investments, but they aren't the best, either. Yet BOARDWALK and PARK PLACE monopoly are designer brands, and all that glitz will blind you to the numbers.

The real world offers shimmering chimeras that mirror the value structure of the dark blue monopoly. The BOARDWALKS and PARK PLACES of the business world are those ventures that seem like instant home runs, but which can be very elusive to obtain and/or harness and very expensive both to acquire and uphold. So it is prudent to "run the numbers" on every business proposition—even those that appear to be no-brainers.

KNEE-JERK EMOTION

The same emotion jerks the knee of all but the most savvy players when it comes time to consider trading four houses for a hotel. That, of course, is the prestige move, a consummation devoutly to be wished—four little green buildings for a single big red one.

And yet, as we saw in *Lesson 12: The Virtue of Shortage*, trading houses for a hotel is often far from the wisest move. A combination of vanity and the official rules tells us that the object of MONOPOLY is to become "the wealthiest player," to accumulate and to triumph. The unofficial truth, however, appeals far less to vanity. The true object of MONOPOLY, as we learned in *Lesson 16: The* Real *Object of the Game*, is not so much to win, but to force the others to lose.

As play enters its final phases, one of the most effective means of pushing the others out of the game is by creating a housing shortage. Once the bank runs out of houses, no one can build—which is a very good thing for you, if your own monopolies are already reasonably well developed. However, yield to desire by trading houses for hotels, and you end the housing shortage, thereby handing your opponents an opportunity to remain in the game, to cost you money, and, maybe, just maybe, push *you* out.

In the world of opportunity, there is only so much to go around. If you are truly to succeed, make sure you take your opportunities and protect them, and also that you look for ways to scoop others' opportunities.

Chance

The point is that you can't be too greedy.
—Donald J. Trump, American real estate developer

MANAGING EMOTION

Without emotion, there is only motion—or in other words, the meaningless movement of zombie pod-people "doing their jobs" and "performing their functions." It would be foolish to attempt to purge feeling from a great game, and it would be downright tragic to attempt to drain it from life. Nevertheless, it is a valuable gaming and business discipline to develop the faculty of seeing through and looking around emotion when it comes to making the hard decisions about buying, selling, and holding.

Manage your heart. See through your feelings to the fundamental numbers. Look around your emotions to the goal that is fundamental, to the real object of the game.

LESSON 26:

START-UP STRATEGIES

Three strategies will give you an edge at the very start of the game.

THE FIRST START-UP STRATEGY

Begin with a determination to keep track, from the start, of just what's in the game and who has what. This means watching everyone's money and everyone's properties, including your own. It also means knowing the basic elements that reduce the element of chance in MONOPOLY, such as:

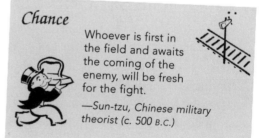

Chance

Whoever is first in the field and awaits the coming of the enemy, will be fresh for the fight.

—Sun-tzu, Chinese military theorist (c. 500 B.C.)

• It usually takes five turns to get around the board.

• Each player will probably roll doubles once each time around the board.

• Each player will probably land on four of the 28 property spaces each time around the board.

Now, early in the game, landing on a property will probably mean an opportunity to buy it. As the game progresses, however, you'll need to start anticipating the consequences of landing on someone else's property. We'll get into this in the next lesson.

Start keeping track of the CHANCE and COMMUNITY CHEST cards from the beginning. These are never shuffled in the course of the game, and there are only sixteen CHANCE and sixteen COMMUNITY CHEST cards, so you should try to anticipate what cards are going to come up. Watch which ones come up in the first moves of the game. Get an idea of their order. Then, by the time the opening phase of the game dissolves into the middle game, you should be able to anticipate what cards will come up. It doesn't take a Vegas card counter to get a feel for the flow of these two decks of sixteen cards.

Go into the game knowing the odds of throwing any number with the dice. (For odds calculations, see *Lesson 3: A Roll of the Dice.*)

Similarly, when approaching a new business venture outside the board game, you shouldn't take the inital leap until you know the lay of the land. Understanding the whereabouts and availability of all the resources you may need to be successful is the first step towards being successful.

THE SECOND START-UP STRATEGY

Make a mental inventory of what you know about your opponent. Resolve to use this knowledge to your advantage. If you are playing with friends or family, this should be easy. If you've played MONOPOLY with these folks before, summon up what you know about their game. Is Joe impulsive? Is Jill a risk taker? Is Sue conservative? Is Ed timid? Is Pete a casual player or a serious one? Is Sheila aggressive?

And don't forget the advice of the venerable Oracle of Delphi: *Know thyself.* What is *your* style of play? Know it, then play to your strengths and be aware of your weaknesses.

Even if you aren't well acquainted with your opponents, work with whatever information you can gather. For example, consider:

• What does Joe do for a living? Is he a CPA or a professional sky-diver?

• How is Jill dressed? Casual, conservative, daring? Does she wear fun colors, or more on the somber side?

• What token did Pete choose for himself? Take a look at *Lesson 17: Psych (Or, Who's the Shlub Who Chose the Shoe?)*.

The application of this strategy to the real world is fairly obvious. Having an awareness of your competitors' basic character and tendencies gives you an edge in the realm of competition.

THE THIRD START-UP STRATEGY

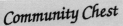

Community Chest

It is better to be impetuous than circumspect.
—Niccolò Machiavelli, 16th century Italian writer and thinker

As Strother Martin's character "advises" Paul Newman's character in the film *Cool Hand Luke*, "You gotta get your mind right."

From the beginning, decide to win. For one, this means resolving to be ethically ruthless, as discussed in Lessons 18, 19, and 20. If you understand and accept the "real" object of MONOPOLY—that is, the total elimination of your opponents—then you will have no trouble being ruthless. For a ruthless approach proceeds directly from that ruthless object. (If you need a refresher on that object, reread *Lesson 16: The* Real *Object of the Game*, before starting play.)

Deciding to win requires getting your energy up. Especially at the beginning of the game, you need to be in an aggressive buying mode. Don't worry about conserving cash at this point. Now is the time to convert cash into property. Remember, you are not *spending* money, but *investing* it. At best, you are striving for an early lead in building monopolies. At the least, each property you acquire now is one less opportunity for another player. The opening of the game is not the time for a casual, studied approach to acquisition. It is time to bare your teeth and gobble up real estate.

Community Chest

Boldness in business is the first, second, and third thing.
—*Thomas Fuller, British physician and philosopher*

As the start-up phase yields to the middle game— this phase comes when any player successfully completes a monopoly—you may begin to be more selective about acquiring real estate. We'll cover the principles of such selectivity in the next lesson.

RELATIONSHIPS

In MONOPOLY, trading with other players is important—more important than most players think (see *Lesson 13: Let's Talk*). In the opening phases of the game, trade whenever you can advantageously acquire a property; however, now is not the time to create alliances or to "gang up" on another player. Not only is it too early to evaluate the strategic value of any given alliance, it is impossible for such an alliance to *have* a strategic value. In the early part of the game, there are just too many properties available to everyone. Grabbing as many of these as possible should be your focus, and prematurely allying yourself with another player will just get in the way.

Alliances forged during the opening moves are not created out of strategic motives, but because one player happens to like Opponent A more than Opponent B. In MONOPOLY, alliances should be made only when doing so improves your position in the game; this does not become feasible until well into the middle game and, even more so, during the endgame. Right now, it's every player for him or herself.

AND THE GREATEST OF THESE . . .

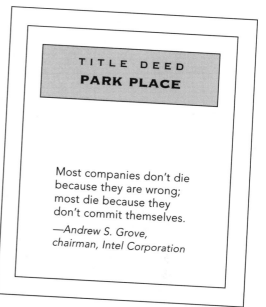

TITLE DEED
PARK PLACE

Most companies don't die because they are wrong; most die because they don't commit themselves.
—*Andrew S. Grove, chairman, Intel Corporation*

In the *New Testament*, the apostle Paul proclaims, "And now abideth faith, hope, charity, these three; but the greatest of these is charity." In Lesson 26 of *Everything I Know about Business I Learned from* MONOPOLY, the things that abideth are gaining knowledge, resolving to keep track of play, learning as much as you can about your opponents, and starting out with your "mind right" in the absolute determination to win.

But the greatest of these is the determination to win.

Without a winning attitude, keeping track of play and knowing your opponents will count for very little indeed. On the other hand, it is precisely by gaining knowledge, staying in control, evaluating the competition, and generally doing whatever you can to reduce the apparent randomness of play that you will gain the confidence to support that all-important will to win.

You won't find any discussion of a beginning, middle, and end in the Official Rules of MONOPOLY, but that doesn't mean the game lacks a beginning, a middle, and an end. It has all three, and, what's more to the point, there is a strategic advantage to be enjoyed in knowing when one ends and the next begins. Such knowledge allows you to tailor your strategy to whatever stage of the game you are in.

Chance

Planning is as natural to the process of success as its absence is to the process of failure.

—Robin Sieger, British business executive and author

END OF THE BEGINNING, BEGINNING OF THE MIDDLE

As we have seen in the preceding lesson, the opening moves of MONOPOLY are no time for conservatism. They are your best chance to acquire property, to invest your cash, to covert that money into opportunity. The opening strategy, in a nutshell, is to buy, buy, buy.

In MONOPOLY, opportunity is defined chiefly by the acquisition of monopolies. Therefore, a monopoly is opportunity crystallized.

At the moment a player builds the first monopoly in the game, the opening game ends, and the middle game begins. The building of the first monopoly marks the transition from equal opportunity for all to decreasing opportunity for some. The building of the first monopoly brings to an end an economy based on plenty and introduces one increasingly based on scarcity.

RECOGNIZING CHANGE

Few businesses, perhaps none, exist in an unchanging environment. Tastes change, technology progresses, needs develop, needs recede, money gets looser, money gets tighter, people feel one thing one day, one year, one decade, and then they feel something else a little later. Markets develop, grow, mature, and, typically, stop growing.

The business environment changes, as does the business itself. There is a start-up period, followed by a period of growth, and then of adaptation—of selective growth and selective retrenchment. Finally comes a period of diversification or one of specialization.

Community Chest

Planning is good, but not if it excludes the opportunity to be able to take chances when they come up.

—Chris Wright, 1998, British entrepreneur

PROFITING BY THE RECOGNITION

Externally and internally, the context of any enterprise changes and develops. The success of the enterprise depends on how nimbly and creatively the people of that enterprise adapt to the changes, anticipating them whenever possible, so that they can be profitably exploited. This requires business leaders who know where they are in time and space, who understand where their enterprise is (start up, growing, mature) and who understand the phase of the markets they serve (start up, growth, mature).

The phases of play in MONOPOLY model, to a limited but significant degree, the changing environment of business. The winning player is typically aware of the current stage of play, and she gears her strategy accordingly.

TIME FOR KNOWLEDGE

In the opening phase of MONOPOLY, your strategy should be focused almost 100 percent on acquisition. Increasingly throughout the middle game, you will want to be more selective in how you invest your cash. In the opening moves, money is an offensive weapon. By the middle game, it must also serve a defensive purpose, insuring that you'll be able to pay the rents demanded of you, so that you can stay in the game, demanding, in turn, rents from others.

Recall from the previous lesson that it generally takes five turns to go around the board. Each trip around, there's a good chance that you'll roll doubles once. Odds are that you'll land on 4 of the 28 property spaces. As those spaces are bought by others, they are—from your perspective—transformed from opportunities into liabilities.

Now is definitely *not* the time to become ultraconservative or timid. Keep buying. However, also keep an eye on your cash. Anticipate what rents you are likely to have to pay as you round the board. You can do this by counting the number of unmortgaged properties your opponents own. Divide this total by 7. The figure that results is a prediction of how many rents you can reasonably expect to pay on your next trip around. Let's say your opponents own a total of 9 properties. Nine divided by 7 is about 1.28. Rounding this off, you can expect to pay at least one rent on your next circuit of the board.

By anticipating the likely demands on your cash, you can make more informed investment decisions. Unless you believe you are long on cash, consider, in the middle game, passing up the cheapest properties, the deep purples and the light blues. Exercise patience to acquire more productive investments—or refrain from buying when you land on the weaker properties, but do remain open to acquiring them at auction for a bargain price. Remember, even the player who declines to buy a property he's landed on is eligible to bid for it.

During the middle game, your knowledge of the relative value of each property color group becomes increasingly important as conserving at least some cash becomes a heightened priority. The "Tip Sheets" in Orbanes's *The MONOPOLY Companion* as well as the information you'll find at the official MONOPOLY web site (www.monopoly.com) are most valuable as you get deeper into a stage of the game that calls for weighing each investment decision.

RULES OF THUMB

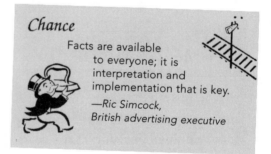

Chance

Facts are available to everyone; it is interpretation and implementation that is key.
—Ric Simcock, British advertising executive

Just don't ponder to the point of paralysis.

In business, when time is relatively plentiful, it pays to invest as much of that commodity as possible in acquiring the best, the most thorough, the most reliable information possible. Often, however, time is in critically short supply and is, as they say, of the essence. Therefore, successful business leaders learn to rely routinely on less than perfect information. They find or they build a body of general rules, rules of thumb, based on experience, hardly infallible, but better than nothing—and, what is more important when time is at a premium, better than *too* much.

As they enter the middle game, experienced MONOPOLY players bring to bear the following rules of thumb concerning property acquisition. *You should always buy if—*

—no other player owns a property in the color group. EXCEPTION: If you are short of cash or facing heavy-duty monopolies, think twice before grabbing up the dark purples and the light blues.

—you already own one or two properties of the color group. If you own one property in the color group, do almost anything to get a shot at a monopoly. If you own two properties in the color group, move heaven and earth to complete the monopoly.

—you can block an opponent from completing a monopoly. This assumes the opponent has two properties in a color group. See *Lesson 5: The Rule of Opportunity*, for a discussion of what to do if an opponent owns only one property in the group or if two opponents each own one property in a color group.

TIME TO TRADE

Chance

Don't just play the game, change the rules.

—Raymond Smith, chairman, Rothschild North America, Inc.

In the middle game, trading among players becomes increasingly important. There are two reasons for this. First, trading is a way of putting yourself in a position to build monopolies that would otherwise be unavailable. Second, as the middle game progresses, the advantages of creating trade-based alliances become more apparent. In the middle game, working with another player to put the squeeze on a third becomes a feasible tactic. See *Lesson 13: Let's Talk* for a discussion of player-to-player trading.

As important as trading is in the middle game, it will be crucial in the endgame, so now is also a good time to prepare for that by creating trade relationships and by establishing the general precedent of trading.

END OF THE MIDDLE, BEGINNING OF THE END

Why is trading so important in the endgame? Simple. The middle game ends and the endgame begins when there are no more potential monopolies left on the board—that is, when it is no longer possible to build a monopoly by landing on an unowned property. Any monopoly built in the endgame is the result of a trade or the bankruptcy of one of the players. We turn to this most interesting phase of the game in the next lesson.

The endgame begins when no more potential monopolies are left on the board. In other words, the start of the endgame comes when it is no longer possible to build a monopoly by landing on an unowned property. Many players mistakenly interpret "endgame" as a synonym for "end of the game." They feel that all of the opportunities are gone and that, now, the game simply "plays itself out." The player or players holding the best monopolies just sit and wait for the cash to come to papa as the other player or players trudge wearily around the board until, one after the other, they fall.

If the contest is a close one, with monopolies pretty evenly distributed, the endgame is typically viewed as strictly a matter of chance. Will you land on your opponent's BOARDWALK before she lands on your PENNSYLVANIA AVENUE?

In either case, most players view the endgame as flying on automatic pilot without much opportunity or need for input. This is a mistake.

ENDGAME DEALS

Experienced players understand that matches can be won or lost in the endgame. They understand that, with the board options used up, the endgame is an exciting, highly charged time for player-to-player trades and alliances.

Focus on the player who's on the ropes. Deal for property he holds and that you need. If you can control just one more monopoly in the endgame, your ability to dominate the others grows significantly.

Community Chest

In our industry, some people are afraid of us because were so good.

—Bill Gates, founder and chairman, Microsoft

Directing your attention to the struggling player is also important defensively. Deal with him for property that will block stronger opponents from trading up to a monopoly.

A word of caution: In your trading with the nearly down-and-out, resist the temptation to be magnanimous. In the first place, making an alliance with a player who's hanging on by his teeth will not give you much bang for your buck. If you are going to gang up on a player to squeeze him out, you want a strong ally—one who owns valuable monopolies and who's willing to give you what you need by way of trade. Even more important, you don't want to bail out a player who is about to be eliminated from the game. Each player out is a step toward winning.

One of the greatest challenges of the endgame is deciding who to trade with, what to trade, and how much to pay. Trade with a struggling opponent only if it will net you a monopoly property. Avoid being charitable. Your object is not to rescue the other player, but to gain more power for yourself. At most, the deal should give the other player a brief reprieve while netting you a significant advantage. You have nothing to gain from keeping an opponent in the game any longer than absolutely necessary.

You've also got to be careful making endgame trades with powerful players. They are not likely to give you a monopoly except at an exorbitant, perhaps ruinous, cost or to create an alliance against another player. The first alternative is almost certainly a poor gamble. If you drain your cash, you may put yourself out of the game. At the very least, you'll find yourself with a monopoly, but no money to develop it. On the other hand, if you can persuade the other player that an alliance will be mutually advantageous, this is your best shot at the leverage you need to strike a reasonable bargain for a monopoly-making property.

In talking to your prospective trading partner, emphasize the benefit to him. Avoid talking about money. Let *him* come up with a number first. In any negotiation, the first person who mentions a figure is thereby put in the weaker bargaining position.

In general, if you have a choice, trade for properties that are close to FREE PARKING. In terms of frequency percentage and return on investment, these are the dynamos, and owning a monopoly in this location late in the game gives you potent dominating power.

EXPLOITING SCARCITY

While reading this lesson and thinking about the endgame, now is the time to take a quick glance back at *Lesson 12: The Virtue of Shortage.* The bank never runs out of money. In a pinch, the Banker just writes the necessary denominations on blank sheets of paper—quite without danger of going to jail, going directly to jail, for counterfeiting. In contrast to cash, houses are a finite commodity in MONOPOLY. Once the Bank runs out of them, there are no more to be had.

The opening moves of MONOPOLY are governed by potential opportunity. The closing moves are dominated by scarcity. But scarcity can be as strong an ally as opportunity. Block opponents from developing their monopolies by doing what you can to create a housing shortage. In the endgame, do not exchange houses for hotels if the Bank is short on houses

Community Chest

When you set the bar at some crazy number with no idea how to get there, you can't believe the results.

—*Jack Welch, former CEO, General Electric*

and your opponents have minimally developed monopolies. If you replenish the Bank's supply of houses, you give your opponents the opportunity to develop their investments and thereby hurt you.

Offensively, the obvious endgame strategy is to build up your most costly monopolies—the kind that really, really hurt when an opponent lands on them. That's fine, but don't be tempted to neglect defense at this stage. If you can create a housing shortage by building extravagantly on your low-rent monopolies, do so.

A TIME FOR VIGILANCE

Far from allowing yourself to fall into the feeling that the endgame can fly on automatic pilot, now is the time to adopt heightened, coffee-nerved vigilance.

Watch the action. Keep track of the CHANCE and COMMUNITY CHEST cards. Keep track of everyone's money and property. Watch the board. How are you going to feel if a player lands on *your* NEW YORK AVENUE with three houses, and *you* forget to demand your rent?

HUSBAND YOUR RESOURCES

Watch your cash and other assets, especially single (non-monopoly) properties you can mortgage to raise cash. Unless you see yourself in an all-or-nothing scenario, with the opportunity to financially destroy an opponent critically short of cash, restrain your own building so that you are left with sufficient assets to cover probable, predictable expenses. (See the previous lesson for the mathematics of accurately predicting your liabilities each time around the board.)

Early in the game, when there are no monopolies against you, all you need to hold on to is $150, perhaps $200. By the start of the middle game, assuming one monopoly is against you, you'll need to retain at least $300. On-hand cash requirements rise from here, as more monopolies are arrayed against you.

As in the real business world, the flow of capital and the availability of liquid assets are relative needs. It's a wise business leader who understands when these needs rise and decline.

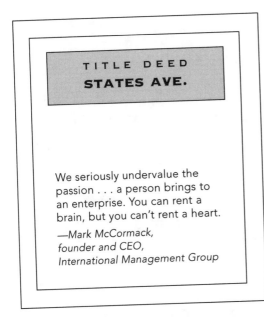

TITLE DEED

STATES AVE.

We seriously undervalue the passion . . . a person brings to an enterprise. You can rent a brain, but you can't rent a heart.
—*Mark McCormack,
founder and CEO,
International Management Group*

PLAN TO BUILD, BUILD TO PLAN

Late-game development of your monopolies should not be random. There is a big jump in rent between monopoly properties with two houses and those with three. Moving from two to three houses represents a high value, a most significant bang for the buck. Therefore, put three houses on each property of your highest-probability monopoly *before* you start building up the next-best monopolies. You want the quickest, biggest return on your investment *now*, in the endgame, when every move counts; therefore, focus on your best monopoly first and bring it to its best value—three houses.

After getting to three houses on your best monopoly, start developing your other properties. Only when these also are brought to the three-house level should you add a fourth house to the properties of your best monopoly. If you can afford to put a fourth house on only one property, put it on the highest-rent property in the group.

Exercise self-control. Your temptation, for example, will be to put hotels on BOARDWALK and PARK PLACE before developing your orange monopoly. You are much better off getting the oranges to the three-house level before sinking most of your resources into the dark blues. And remember: don't thoughtlessly turn in your houses for hotels if doing so will end a housing shortage and give your opponents the opportunity to build.

This said, do be flexible. Don't rigidly and absolutely avoid trading up to hotels. After all, hotels are the only way to make the lowest-rent properties (the dark purples, the light blues, and the light purples) pay significantly. But do avoid trading up in the case of a critical housing shortage when your opponents need desperately to build. Keep them desperate.

This model applies equally to the businessperson who holds many ventures as well as the owners of a Mom and Pop shop. Whatever your most profitable venture or item may be, spend the proper amount of resources building it up. Before you can do that, of course, you need to understand exactly where your bread is buttered. Successful business leaders understand this need.

MORTGAGE VALUE

That collection of single properties gathering dust at the end of the game—properties that never blossomed into monopolies—are not to be neglected now. They may be traded or sold, of course, but they are also important for their mortgage value, to raise needed cash. Review *Lesson 7: Mortgaging the Future* for tips on how, when, what, and why to mortgage.

In the endgame, many players think of their mortgage-ripe properties as insurance, a means of hanging in the game after you're hit by a big-time rent. That is a sound policy, but don't let it rule out mortgaging properties in the endgame to finance building up to three houses on your best monopolies. It's come to this: now or never. *Now* is the time to develop the monopolies that will squeeze your opponents right out of the game.

In essence, timing is everything.

MAKE THE MOST OF A NARROW WORLD

Who doesn't like plenty? Plenty of opportunity. Plenty of everything. Who isn't threatened or, at least, dismayed by scarcity? Dwindling opportunity. The short supply of everything.

At the start of a MONOPOLY game, opportunity abounds. The title deeds are stacked neatly in the bank, waiting. Houses and hotels are plentiful, waiting. And you, you have $1,500, all unspent, all unspoken for.

In the endgame, the MONOPOLY world seems suddenly much narrower. Opportunities are limited. You may hold a number of monopolies, but others, perhaps collectively, may hold more. You have less room to maneuver.

Community Chest

The endgame is just the beginning.
—Pat Croce, American entrepreneur

Well, stop focusing on yourself. Look around you. The world has narrowed not just on you, but on everyone. This is the environment now, and if you don't abandon yourself to chance, the luck of the draw, if you don't relinquish the controls to auto pilot, you can use the narrowness of the endgame to your advantage.

With diminished opportunity comes a reduction in the number of unknowns and variables. The world of the endgame is actually easier to control than the environment of the start-up and the middle. When there's less to grab, it's easier to grab it—if you know how. Grab it.

No matter how much even the most dedicated Monopolist would like to play the game during every free hour, sometimes you have to do something else. Like what? Well, like play the favorite-movie-line game.

We've all done it among friends. You begin to swap classic lines from movies. What's your favorite all-time classic? Let's see, there's "Frankly, my dear, I don't give a damn," from *Gone with the Wind*. Or from *The Graduate*, "I've got just one word for you: *plastics*." There's *Casablanca*'s "Here's looking at you, kid," and from *Taxi Driver*, "Are you lookin' at me?" Don't forget the realm of science fiction and the immortal line Michael Rennie speaks in *The Day the Earth Stood Still*: "Klaatu, berada nikto."

Chance

Monopoly is business at the end of its journey.
—Henry Demarest Lloyd, American journalist and reformer

HARD TO STOP

And so on, and so on. Once you get going, it's hard to stop. But before we do, let's recall these memorable words from 1987's *Wall Street*, which issued from the lips of corporate raider Gordon Gecko (played by Michael Douglas): "Greed, for lack of a better term, greed is good."

Those words, put into the mouth of a film character, were actually paraphrased from the real-life Wall Streeter Ivan Boesky, who went to prison and paid $100 million in fines for violating insider-trading laws. Before all that unpleasantness, he addressed the graduating class of the School of Business Administration at the University of California, Berkeley, on May 18, 1986.

Chance

Monopoly is a terrible thing, till you have it.

—Rupert Murdoch, CEO, News Corporation

"Greed," he told the graduates, "is all right, by the way. I think greed is healthy. You can be greedy and feel good about yourself."

In fairness to Boesky, he was not alone in his advocacy of the gospel of greed. We can go back at least as far as the great nineteenth-century evolutionist Charles Darwin, who told us that nature was not some softhearted, selfless commune, but was (as Alfred, Lord Tennyson put it) "red in tooth and claw," a realm in which only the fittest survive. A few years later, the social philosopher Herbert Spencer applied this notion to society, and from the Darwinian doctrine that only the fittest survive in nature, he declared that much the same was true in so-called civilized society. From this "social Darwinism," it is a very short leap indeed to the Gecko formula, "Greed is good."

THE ENGINE OF GREED

Or maybe that leap, short as it is, isn't quite warranted. Perhaps the point is not that *greed is good*, but that *greed is necessary*: a powerful biological and social engine.

Does greed succeed in driving MONOPOLY victory?

Yes, as a matter of fact, it does.

TWO WORDS

Consider two words: *greed* and *monopoly*. They are, both of them, inflammatory, in that they go against the morality that most of us have been raised to respect. The context of that morality is multifaceted: religious, social, ethical, political, and legal. Now, precisely because *greed* and *monopoly* are inflammatory, they are also, like many other "dirty" words connoting "forbidden" concepts, titillating. This is why Gordon Gecko's phrase stands out as a classic movie line. "Greed is good" is outrageous, yet it also rings with an undeniable truth.

This is also why MONOPOLY is one of the greatest names ever attached to a game. It is compelling and, well, titillating. We are, most of us, fiercely resentful of monopolies in real life. In 1894, workers staged a spectacular strike against the Pullman Palace Car Company, because wages were cut 25 percent while the rents in Pullman-owned houses

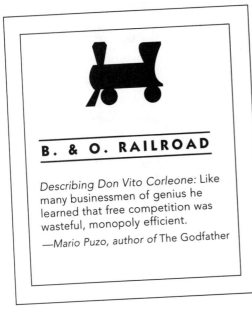

B. & O. RAILROAD

Describing Don Vito Corleone: Like many businessmen of genius he learned that free competition was wasteful, monopoly efficient.
—Mario Puzo, author of The Godfather

and Pullman-owned apartments and the prices in Pullman-owned stores remained fixed. Pullman had a local monopoly on housing and retail goods. The people were prisoners of Pullman, and the situation was evil; undeniably it was monopoly at its worst. Today, many of us still rail at cable TV monopolies, at software vendor monopolies, and, depending where we live, at a host of other monopolies.

A NAUGHTY NOTION

Chance

If you have an olive, you want an olive tree. You want a little more. You want the whole tree.

—Ted Turner, founder, Turner Broadcasting System

And yet, who wouldn't like to have a monopoly of one's own? To possess all the goodies? To control everything everybody needed or wanted?

It's a naughty notion, to be sure, but naughty notions are the ones that are the most fun. MONOPOLY lets us play naughty. The object of this game is not to build businesses or create business excellence. It is to build monopolies that add up to the ultimate monopoly, the monopoly to end all monopolies: a world in which only you are left standing.

The appeal, purpose, and pleasure of a great game is that it simultaneously models some aspect of real life even as it creates a "play area" apart from real life. And MONOPOLY is a great game. It models business life in an astounding variety of ways. Yet it is on the essential point of MONOPOLY—the goal of the game, the name of the game—that the model falls apart and real life makes way for play.

GAME OVER

As the preceding lessons have shown, MONOPOLY embodies many skills, values, and concepts that drive and inform successful business. However, *monopoly*, as a synonym for *victory* in this game, is not among those skills, values, and concepts.

In real life, if you are the only one standing, you are out of business, along with everybody else. MONOPOLY, in its purest form, the form that ends the game, is the end of business. In the year 280 B.C., Pyrrhus, king of Epirus, defeated a Roman army at the Battle of Heraclea. It was a great victory, yet one achieved at a staggering cost to his forces. Congratulated on his triumph, Pyrrhus replied, "One more such victory and I shall be lost." Ever since, we have spoken of a "Pyrrhic victory" as one not worth winning. Such, in real life, is a business monopoly.

Taken to its ultimate, a monopoly does not just eliminate competitors. It eliminates everyone. A total monopoly creates conditions that make business impossible or not worth the doing, which comes to the same thing. Do you need an example of a total monopoly in real life? Look at the sad, smoldering heap that was once the Soviet Union, built on the sand of a government monopoly known as a demand economy.

In the game of MONOPOLY, monopoly ends the game. We call that winning. Viewed as a model of real-life business, however, it is the ultimate defeat, and it is so precisely because it *ends the game.*

Community Chest

What kind of society isn't structured on greed?

—Milton Friedman, American economist

In MONOPOLY, winning is making the other players lose. That is the unofficial but nevertheless quite real definition of winning in this game. As with any other game, winning MONOPOLY requires ending the game. In business, making the others lose likewise ends the game, but that brings defeat or a Pyrrhic victory, which, not worth the winning, is the bottom-line equivalent of defeat.

BREAKDOWN

Because winning in MONOPOLY is losing in real life, we must say that here, at this point, MONOPOLY and real life part company. That is as it should be. MONOPOLY is not, first and last, a business model. First and last, it is a *game*—which, along the way, happens to model business, often amazingly well. But in the breakdown, the parting of game and reality, may be found perhaps the most profound business lesson of MONOPOLY. It is this: Games end in defeat and victory. Business can end in neither.

Where, then, is victory in business? Winning is the continuation, the perpetuation, the *non-ending* of business.

What must you do to succeed in business? You must repeatedly and continually devise means by which the game never ends.

Will everybody *win*? Not likely. But winning in business is the delicate art of creating conditions in which there are just enough winners at any given time and at all times to keep the game going, to keep you in business, and to keep your business growing. *That* is the limit of greed.

SOURCE INDEX

Sources for the quotations included in this book are listed below by page number.

PART I – There Are Rules

13. Watson, Thomas Sr. (*Father, Son & Co.: My Life at IBM and Beyond*)

15. Roberts, Len (author interview)

16. Peskaitis, Steve (from businessweek.com)

18. Ernst, Mark A. (author interview)

22. Eccleston, Bernie (from the book *The Business of Winning*)

23. Hill, Damon (from the *Sunday Times*, London)

24. Boesky, Ivan (from the *Times*, London)

24. Roberts, Len (author interview)

26. Blanchard, Kenneth (The One Minute Manager)

26. Jobs, Steve (interview with Daniel Morrow of the Computerworld Smithsonian Awards Program)

27. Peter, Lawrence J. (*Why Things Go Wrong: The Peter Principle Revisited*)

28.   Cuban, Mark (ESPN interview)

29.   Tarantino, Dominic (commencement address, McLaren Business School, University of San Francisco, 1995)

32.   Buffet, Warren (from the book *Business*)

33.   Ernst, Mark A. (author interview)

34.   England, Donald (from *Fortune* magazine)

36.   Sloan, Alfred P. (from the book *Corporate Cultures*)

40.   Luby, Dallas (from *Investor's Business Daily*)

41.   Parkinson, C. Northcote (from the book *The Monopoly Companion*)

42.   Orbanes, Philip (*The Monopoly Companion*)

43.   Murchison, Clint W. (from Time magazine)

44.   Forbes, Bill (from the book *The Monopoly Companion*)

45.   Hammer, Armand (*Witness to History*)

46.   Robertson, Heather (*Taking Care of Business*)

47.   Branson, Richard (from the *Broad Street Journal*)

49.   Birdseye, Clarence (from *American Magazine*)

51.   Sculley, John (from *Fortune* magazine)

52.   Adams, Scott (*The Dilbert Principle*)

53.   Kiyosaki, Robert T. (*Rich Dad, Poor Dad*)

54.   Ernst, Mark A. (author interview)

56.   Goizueta, Roberto (from *Fortune* magazine)

58.   Dulles, John Foster (from *Life* magazine)

59.   Adams, Scott (*The Dilbert Principle*)

61.   Welch, Jack (from the *Harvard Business Review*)

62.   Quant, Mary (from *The Observer*, London)

65.   Sloan, Alfred P. (*My Years with General Motors*)

67.   Calloway, Wayne (from *Fortune* magazine)

68.   Peters, Tom (*A Passion for Excellence*)

69.   Murdoch, Rupert (from the book *Murdoch*)

70.   Peter, Lawrence J. (*The Peter Principle: Why Things Always Go Wrong*)

71.   Sun-tzu (*The Art of War*)

74.   Roberts, Len (author interview)

75.   Kelleher, Herb (from *Nation'sBusiness* magazine)

77.   Einstein, Albert

79.   De Vries, Peter (from the *Washington Post*)

81.   Rogers, Will (from *The Illiterate Digest*)

82.   Goizueta, Roberto (from *Fortune* magazine)

84.   Weill, Sanford I. (from lippincott-margulies.com)

85.   Carnegie, Dale (*How to Win Friends and Influence People*)

85.   Goizueta, Roberto (from *Fortune* magazine)

86.   Grove, Andrew S. (*Only the Paranoid Survive*)

87.   Eio, Peter (commencement address, Western New England College, 1993)

88.   Kettering, Charles Franklin (from *Reader's Digest* magazine)

89.   Kiam, Victor (from the *East Valley Tribune*)

90.   Jacobs, Greg (from the book *The Monopoly Companion*)

91.   Firestone, Harvey (*Men and Rubber*)

92.   Cummings, William (from cummings.com)

93.   Porter, Michael (from the *Economist*)

95.   Brodow, Ed (*Negotiate with Confidence*)

96.   Getty, J. Paul (from the book *Getty on Getty*)

97.   Zeldin, Theodore (*An Intimate History of Humanity*)

98.   Kiam, Victor (*Going for It*)

99.   Yamani, Sheik Ahmed Zaki (from the book *Yamani*)

101.   Ernst, Mark A. (author interview)

104.   Getty, J. Paul (from the *International Herald Tribune*)

105.   Icahn, Carl C. (from *Fortune* magazine)

106.   Horlick, Nicola (*Can You Have It All?*)

107.   Diller, Barry (from *Business Week*)

108.   Borman, Frank (from the book *Business*)

109.   Steinbrenner, George (from the *New York Times*)

110.   Eisner, Michael (from the book *Business*)

111.   Hadfield, Bud (*Wealth within Reach*)

PART II – And Then There Are *Your* Rules

115.   Vidal, Gore (from the book *Business*)

116.   Revson, Charles (from *Time* magazine)

118.   Kroc, Ray (from the book *Big Mac)*

119.   Grade, Lew (from *You Magazine*)

120.   Terman, Dana (from the book *The Monopoly Companion*)

122. Cuban, Mark (ESPN interview)

124. Joronen, Liisa (from the book *The Winning Streak Mark II*)

125. Smith, Raymond (from *Fortune* magazine)

126. Woo, Christopher (from the book *The Monopoly Companion*)

127. Juran, Joseph M. (from juran.com)

129. Ash, Mary Kay (from the *New York Times*)

130. Soros, George (from a speech at the World Economic Forum, 2000)

131. Joseph, Kenneth (*The Limits of Organization*)

131. Morgan, J. P. (from a statement before the U.S Congress)

132. Ali, Muhammed (from the *New York Times*)

133. Rothschild, Baron (*The Whims of Fortune*)

134. Packer, Kerry (from the *Daily Mail*, London)

135. Onassis, Aristotle (from the *Sunday Times*, London)

136. Kroc, Ray (from the *Wall Street Journal*)

136. Forrester, Lynn (from the *Sunday Times*, London)

138: Ernst, Mark A. (author interview)

139. Mizner, Wilson (from the book *The Legendary Mizners*)

141. Sparrow, Gerald (*How to Become a Millionaire*)

143. Eisner, Michael (from moneysearch.com)

146. Ohmae, Kenichi (*The Mind of the Strategist*)

147. Gracian, Baltasar (from the book *Business*)

148. Ecker, Frederick Hudson (from the *New York Times*)

149. Kiyosaki, Robert T. (*Rich Dad, Poor Dad*)

151.   Cocteau, Jean (from the book *Business*)

153.   Boesky, Ivan (from the *Wall Street Journal*)

154:    Jobs, Steve (from hotwired.com)

156.   Gates, Bill (from cnn.com)

158.   Moore, Chris (from *Marketing* magazine)

159.   Farris, Paul and Pfeifer, Phil (from a paper at the Darden Graduate School of Business, University of Virginia)

160.   Forbes, Steve (from *Reason* magazine)

161.   Dell, Michael (from *Fast Company Magazine*)

162.   Branson, Richard (from *Red Herring Magazine*)

163.   Buffet, Warren (from *Fortune* magazine)

164.   Koch, Charles G. (from *Imprimis* magazine)

165.   Arden, Elizabeth (from the book *In Cosmetics the Old Mystique is No Longer Enough*)

166.   Shehadie, Sir Nicholas (from the *Sydney Morning Herald*)

168.   Armour, Philip D. (from *Forbes* magazine)

169.   Hadfield, Bud (*Wealth within Reach*)

170.   rady, Charles (from the *Sunday Times*, London)

171.   Trump, Donald J. (*Trump: The Art of the Deal*)

173.   Sun-tzu (*The Art of War*)

175.   Machiavelli, Niccolo (*The Prince*)

176.   Fuller, Thomas (*Gnomologia*)

177.   Grove, Andrew S. (*Only the Paranoid Survive*)

178.   Sieger, Robin (*Natural Born Winners*)

179. Wright, Chris (from the book *The Adventure Capitalists*)

181. Simcock, Ric (from *Marketing* magazine)

182. Smith, Raymond (from *Fortune* magazine)

185. Gates, Bill (from Playboy magazine)

186. Welch, Jack (from senndelaneyleadership.com)

188. McCormack, Mark (*McCormack on Managing*)

190. Croce, Pat (publisher interview)

192. Lloyd, Henry Demarest (*Wealth agasint Commonwealth*)

193. Murdoch, Rupert (from *The New Yorker* magazine)

194. Puzo, Mario (*The Godfather*)

195. Turner, Ted (from the *New York Times*)

196. Friedman, Milton (*There's No Such Thing as a Free Lunch*)